Assessment Practices and Procedures in Children and Adolescents with Traumatic Brain Injury

Stephen R. Hooper, Ph.D.
Department of Allied Health Sciences
University of North Carolina School of Medicine

Item: APPC

Copyright © 2013 by Stephen Hooper

All rights reserved. No part of this book may be reproduced, stored in a retrieval system, or transmitted in any form or by any means, electronic, mechanical, photocopying, recording, or otherwise, except for brief reviews, without the prior written permission of the publisher.

Published by Lash & Associates Publishing/Training Inc.
100 Boardwalk Drive, Suite 150, Youngsville, NC 27596
Tel: (919) 556-0300 Fax: (919) 556-0900

For a free catalog, contact Lash & Associates or visit our website and blog *www.lapublishing.com*

LASH & ASSOCIATES PUBLISHING, INC.

100 BOARDWALK DRIVE, SUITE 150, YOUNGSVILLE, NC 27596 TEL:
(919) 556-0300 FAX: (919) 556-0900

WWW.LAPUBLISHING.COM

TABLE OF CONTENTS

About the Author V
Acknowledgments V
Preface VI

SECTION I: Foundations

Chapter 1 - Introduction to Assessment in Children and Adolescents with Traumatic Brain Injury.........IX
What is Assessment?...1
Definition of Traumatic Brain Injury (TBI)..................1
Altered State of Consciousness..................................2
Degree of Post-Traumatic Amnesia (PTA).................4
Presence of Physical Damage.....................................4
Types of Brain Injuries...5
The Special Condition of Concussion........................6
A Note on Screening for a Traumatic Brain Injury...9
The Need for a Comprehensive Assessment............9

Chapter 2 - Types of Assessment............................11
Neurological Assessment..11
Psychological Assessment..12
Building a Neuropsychological Perspective — The Expanded Assessment...12

Chapter 3 - Neuropsychological Constructs and Expanded Assessment Procedures......................15
Stages of Neuropsychological Assessment............15
Approaches to Neuropsychological Assessment
Boston Process Approach...16
Qualitative Approach...17
Fixed Battery Approach...17
Neuropsychological Construct Models....................18
Lurian Neuropsychological Constructs...................19

SECTION II: Assessment Constructs and Procedures

Chapter 4 - Motor Functions...................................21
Findings in Children and Adolescents with Traumatic Brain Injury..21
Assessment Procedures..22
Lateral Dominance and Handedness......................24
A Cautionary Note...25
Summary...25

Chapter 5 - Sensory Functions................................27
Description..27
Vision...28
Ocular Dominance...28
Visual Impairments..28
Auditory...29
Ear Dominance...30
Auditory Impairments...30
Tactile..31
Olfactory (Smell)..32
Gustatory (Taste)...33
Summary...34

Chapter 6 - Attention Functions.............................35
Description..35
Findings in Children and Adolescents with Traumatic Brain Injury..36
Assessment Procedures..37
Summary...38

Chapter 7 - Language Functions............................39
Description..39
Expressive Language..39
Receptive Language...40
Pragmatic Language..40
Findings in Children and Adolescents with Traumatic Brain Injury..41
Assessment Procedures..42
Summary...43

Chapter 8 - Visual Processing Functions..............45
Description..45
Findings in Children and Adolescents with Traumatic Brain Injury..46
Assessment Procedures..46
Summary...47

Chapter 9 - Memory & Learning Functions.........49
Description..49
Findings in Children and Adolescents with Traumatic Brain Injury..50
Assessment Procedures..52
Summary...54

Chapter 10 - Executive Functions..........55
Description..........55
Findings in Children and Adolescents
with Traumatic Brain Injury..........56
Assessment Procedures..........57
Summary..........60

Chapter 11 - Social & Behavior Functions..........63
Description..........63
Psychiatric Disorders..........63
Dimensional Classification..........63
Neuroaffective Models..........64
Family Factors..........65
Findings in Children and Adolescents
with Traumatic Brain Injury..........65
Psychiatric Disorders..........65
Neuroaffective Processing..........67
Family Functions..........68
Assessment Procedures..........70
Behavioral Observations..........70
Clinical Interviews..........71
Behavior Rating Scales..........72
Neuroaffective Measures..........74
Family Measures..........74
Summary..........75

Chapter 12 - Child Neuropsychological Batteries..........77
Description..........77
Assessment Procedures..........78
Traditional Child Neuropsychological
Batteries..........78
Computerized Neuropsychological
Batteries for Children..........80
Summary..........82

**Chapter 13 - Psychoeducational
Assessment Procedures**..........85
Description..........85
Findings in Children and Adolescents
with Traumatic Brain Injury..........85
Assessment Procedures..........87
Measures of Intellectual Functioning..........87
IQ Short-Forms..........89
Academic Achievement Tests..........90
Summary..........90

SECTION III:
Related Assessment Issues

Chapter 14 - Related Assessment Issues..........93
Collection of All Background Information..........93
Neurodevelopmental Constraints..........94
Communication of Results..........95
Team Evaluations and Approaches..........95
Assessment-Treatment Linkages..........96
Community and School Re-Integration..........97
Legal Ramifications..........98
Prevention..........99
Knowledge, Knowledge, Knowledge..........100

Chapter 15 - Epilogue..........103
Future Directions..........103

References..........107

LASH & ASSOCIATES
PUBLISHING INC
100 BOARDWALK DRIVE, SUITE 150
YOUNGSVILLE, NC 27596
TEL: (919) 556-0300
FAX: (919) 556-0900
WWW.LAPUBLISHING.COM

About the Author

Stephen R. Hooper, Ph.D.

Stephen R. Hooper, Ph.D., is a licensed psychologist in the state of North Carolina with specialty training in child/pediatric neuropsychology. He is the Associate Dean and Chair of the Department of Allied Health Sciences at The University of North Carolina School of Medicine and holds additional appointments as: Professor in the Department of Psychiatry/Clinical Professor in the Department of Pediatrics; Research Professor in the Department of Psychology; Clinical Professor in the School of Education; Fellow at Frank Porter Graham Child Development Institute; and Adjunct Professor in the Department of Psychiatry and Behavioral Sciences at Duke University Medical School. He previously served as the Associate Director and the Director of Education and Training at the Carolina Institute for Developmental Disabilities (CIDD) where he also was the Director of the Child and Adolescent Neuropsychology Consultation Service.

Over the last 27 years, Dr. Hooper has developed an international reputation in the field of child neuropsychology with a focus on neurologically-based disorders, including children and adolescents with acquired brain injuries. He has been actively working with state and national initiatives related to this population and has served on the North Carolina Council for Brain Injury in some capacity since its inception in 1990. He has worked on traumatic brain injury training initiatives with the North Carolina Department of Public Instruction and the Division of Mental Health/Developmental Disabilities/Substance Abuse Services for over 20 years. Most recently, he has become the state Director of the state Pediatric Acquired Brain Injury (PABI) organization.

Dr. Hooper has spent much of his career in a leaderhip capacity, working in interdisciplinary settings devoted to childhood neurological disorders, with a specific focus on assessment practices, assessment-treatment linkages, and community outreach for children and their families.

Acknowledgments

I would like to thank my family for putting up with yet another project that has cluttered the house with my various materials. To Mary, Lindsay, and Madeline, I thank you for your tolerance. Madeline, thank you for taking some of the time out of your summer to assist me with the tedious task of organizing the references for this book. To my brother, John. Thank you for your hospitality and generosity in using your home as a major work space and for the use of your computer and internet services. These resources were invaluable in moving this book forward to completion.

I also would like to thank Marilyn Lash and Bob Cluett for their incredible patience with my other work duties and the subsequent frequent delays that followed. Marilyn and Bob, I hope it was worth the wait.

Finally, I would like to extend a heartfelt thank you to all of the children and families with whom I have worked over the years. You truly have been my teachers and counselors for many parts of this book. As always, any shortcomings of this work remain solely my responsibility.

Preface

Neurological involvement of any kind can have a significant impact on the functioning of a child or adolescent, not to mention the additional rippling effects that can occur in the individual's school, family, and social circles. This is especially true in the case of childhood brain injuries, traumatic or acquired, where the sudden nature of the injury and its severity can alter the developmental progression, expectations, and environmental arena of an individual forever. Indeed, an injury during childhood or adolescence can not only alter the developmental trajectories of many cognitive and social functions in an obvious fashion, but it also can affect functioning in a not-so-obvious fashion.

As an example, the behavioral manifestations of an injury may lay "silent" until developmental demands are placed on those specific functions. In this instance, the actual injury may be long forgotten and its contribution to later difficulties not considered. This may lead to other interpretations suggestive of oppositional behavior, laziness, or lack of interest. Recognition of the possible impact that a brain injury can have on a child in the moment, during recovery, and on future developmental functions is critical. Having an accurate assessment of the sequelae of a brain injury is an essential component of the recovery process. In addition, an accurate and thorough assessment can guide appropriate interventions and suggest ongoing developmental surveillance via related assessment and observational strategies.

When we penned our first book on this topic, *Pediatric Traumatic Brain Injury* (Snow & Hooper, 1994) about 20 years ago, the state of the field was such that little training was offered in this area to professionals in medicine, psychology, education, social work, nursing, or other disciplines where such clients might be evaluated and treated. We predicted that innovative changes would be forthcoming. Unfortunately, despite recent efforts to increase the awareness of brain injuries, such as with our returning war veterans and greater recognition of concussions from sports-related injuries, there has been little forward progress with respect to integrating this information into formal curricula. Even with the changes in federal legislation to include traumatic brain injury as a special education classification under the federal special education law in the early 1990s, few changes to training programs in clinical psychology, school psychology, counseling psychology, social work, or special education have been implemented to increase the knowledge base and clinical competencies of these key professionals. Although programs in speech and language pathology and clinical neuropsychology may have an advantage in their study of brain functions and dysfunctions, even in these programs an emphasis has not been placed on the assessment of children with various types of traumatic brain injuries.

The primary purpose of this book is to focus on psychological assessment practices in the broad area of childhood brain injuries. It was designed to complement many of the other texts in the Lash & Associates' library; consequently, there will be a sole focus on assessment practices, procedures, and related issues. Additionally, while the bulk of the discussion will center on formal standardized assessment tasks, informal measures should always be considered in the assessment process of children who have sustained a traumatic brain injury. Relatedly, this text will provide an overview of many of these standardized procedures and how they may fit into a construct-oriented assessment approach, but in-depth descriptions have been provided in other excellent volumes (e.g., Lezak, Howieson, & Loring, 2004; Strauss, Sherman, & Spreen, 2006), and the interested reader is pointed in the direction of these resources.

Topics devoted to definitional issues and mechanisms, the different types of brain injuries, secondary medical complications, and core brain development are dealt with in other volumes, and will only be alluded to in this book. As such, this book will interest anyone who may engage in the psychological assessment of children and adolescents who have sustained a brain injury. It is designed for professionals, parents, and even consumers who may be interested in the various aspects of assessment following a brain

SECTION I
Foundations

injury, and should serve as a guide for a "paradigm shift" for those evaluators who are entrenched in traditional psychological, behavioral, and/or psychoeducational approaches to assessment.

Children and adolescents who have sustained a brain injury represent a rather unique group of individuals who can make dynamic changes over relatively brief periods of time. Understanding these dynamics of change can facilitate application of a different approach to assessment of strengths and weaknesses, linkages to evidence-based interventions, and prediction of later manifestations of functioning.

This text is divided into three major sections. The first section, Foundations, contains three chapters. Chapter 1 provides a basis for conducting various kinds of assessment with children and adolescents with brain injuries. In particular, this chapter describes a rationale for the book taking a neuropsychological perspective in its approach to assessment. Chapter 2 addresses a few of the different types of assessment that children may receive and includes discussions of neurological, psychological, and neuropsychological assessment. Chapter 3 describes the various approaches to neuropsychological assessment and introduces the notion of neuropsychological constructs as a method for operationalizing a flexible battery, or expanded battery approach to children and adolescents who have sustained a brain injury. It is in this chapter that the basis for a construct approach to assessment is presented which, in turn, sets the stage for the second section of this book.

The second section, Assessment Constructs and Procedures, comprises 10 chapters. Chapters 4 through 10 are devoted to describing a targeted neuropsychological construct, with a focus on the multidimensionality of the construct, specific findings in childhood brain injury, and detailing specific assessment procedures that align with that construct. Specifically, these chapters address the brain functions of motor, sensory, attention, language, visual processing, memory/learning, and executive functions. Chapter 11 deals with the broad area of social-behavioral functions, and highlights the importance of assessing these functions post injury regardless of the nature or severity of the brain insult. Two additional chapters are included in this section. Although not constructs, per se, chapters 12 and 13 briefly describe the child neuropsychological batteries and the psychoeducational tasks—including intellectual measures—that also have multiple assessment constructs embedded within their format. A review of representative batteries and tests within these areas is important in that it is highly likely that these measures will be employed in a flexible or expanded battery approach.

The final section, Related Assessment Issues, contains two chapters. Chapter 14 addresses additional, but important assessment issues that the evaluator or team should be aware of in order to conduct a thorough assessment of a child or adolescent following a brain injury. This includes such topics of related assessment components, such as collecting all background information and communication of evaluation findings, but also topics that could impinge on an assessment, such as neurodevelopmental constraints and legal ramifications. Finally, the book concludes with an Epilogue via Chapter 15. This chapter provides a brief recap of the major issues and themes presented in this volume, but also asserts areas of need for future directions in assessment of children and adolescents following a brain injury.

With this volume, it is hoped that the assessment needs of children and adolescents who have sustained a brain injury can be addressed in a more efficient and competent fashion. Additionally, for the field, it is hoped that this volume will provide guidance to encourage a paradigm shift in how children with brain injuries are assessed and monitored as they move through the process of recovery. In accordance with federal laws and guidelines, it is hoped that more timely and comprehensive assessments will improve the intervention for this population of children so that rehabilitation, educational services, and ultimately human potential can be facilitated. Finally, it is hoped that with improved assessment strategies, the chances of poor outcomes for children and families secondary to lack of services or poor services are lessened.

Chapter 1
Introduction to Assessment in Pediatric Traumatic Brain Injury

What is Assessment?

How does one define assessment? One basic definition notes that it is the "act of assessing or appraising," such as one might do with a student's achievement. Another definition defines assessment as "a goal directed problem solving process that uses various measures within a theoretical framework. It is a variable process that depends on the questions asked, the type of student, and a myriad of social, developmental, and contextual factors. It cannot be reduced to a finite set of steps or rules."

Both definitions would be appropriate for application to children and adolescents with traumatic brain injury. The first one provides the basic notion of describing a current level of status, whereas the second one provides the clinical venue for asking and answering clinical questions as they relate to a particular child's needs.

The latter definition is particularly useful for children and adolescents who have sustained a brain injury as there will be constant questions and challenges that will require specific types of assessment to gain an accurate appraisal of that child's needs.

This chapter provides an introduction of the measurement issues inherent in the various definitions of traumatic brain injury and related acquired brain injuries (ABI). It describes the need for conducting comprehensive assessments of the cognitive, academic, and social-behavioral needs of many children following a brain injury.

Definitions of Traumatic Brain Injury or TBI

Over 25 years ago, the National Head Injury Foundation (1985) defined a traumatic brain injury (TBI) as:

An insult to the brain, not of a degenerative or congenital nature, but caused by an external force that produces a diminished or altered state of consciousness

This definition is quite straightforward, and contains the basic factors important to identifying a traumatic brain injury. First, there must be an external force. This does not necessarily entail physical contact, although in many instances it does via some type of blow to the head. Second, the definition is clear to note that some type of change must be present following the exposure to the external force beginning with a diminished or altered state of consciousness and associated cognitive and/or behavioral manifestations.

The same organization, now the Brain Injury Association of America (Brain Injury of American Board of Directors, 2011; http://biausa.org), more recently defined traumatic brain injury, or TBI, as:

...an alteration in brain function, or other evidence of brain pathology, caused by an external force.

The Brain Injury Association of America (Brain Injury of American Board of Directors, 2011; http://biausa.org) also defined an acquired brain injury, or ABI, as:

...an injury to the brain, which is not hereditary, congenital, degenerative, or induced by birth trauma. An acquired brain injury is an injury to the brain that has occurred after birth.

Acquired brain injuries typically include those that are "non-traumatic." Specific examples of acquired brain injury can be seen in individuals who experience stroke, near drowning, hypoxic or anoxic events, tumors, exposure to neurotoxins, electrical shock, or lightning strikes.

These more contemporary definitions do not include all of the core components of their predecessor, but the inclusion of impairments in cognitive, physical, and emotional/behavioral functioning as critical to understanding and defining traumatic brain injury is implied by the definition. Importantly, the definition of traumatic brain injury is now more tightly linked to acquired brain injury in that TBI is viewed as a subset of ABI.

Other definitions have proliferated, such as the one generated by the National Institutes of Health, but the one that has had the largest impact on school functioning has come from the Individuals with Disabilities Education Act (IDEA, U.S. Office of Education, 1992), and its subsequent reauthorizations. An interagency committee composed of representatives from the National Head Injury Foundation, Office of Special Education and Rehabilitation Services, Council of State Administrators of Vocational Rehabilitation, and the National Association of State Directors of Special Education was organized in 1985 to promote the recognition and expansion of services to individuals who had sustained traumatic brain injuries.

It was the efforts of this collaborative group that spawned the IDEA legislation. The IDEA legislation, formerly known as the Education of the Handicapped Act, was signed into law in the fall of 1990 and amended the definition of children with disabilities to include children with brain injuries. In addition, this legislation mandated traumatic brain injury as a new exceptional children's classification. This definition, and those included in subsequent reauthorizations, defined traumatic brain injury or TBI as:

An acquired injury to the brain caused by an external physical force, resulting in total/partial disability or psychological impairment, or both, that adversely affects a child's educational performance. The term applies to open or closed head injuries, resulting in impairments in one or more areas, such as cognition; language; memory; attention; reasoning; abstract thinking; judgment; problem solving; sensory, perceptual, and motor abilities; psychosocial behavior; physical functions; information processing; and speech. The term does not apply to brain injuries that are congenital or degenerative, or brain injuries induced by birth trauma.

This definition includes the issues of injury mechanism, but explains the "altered state of consciousness" in more detail. Not only does this definition implicate an interdisciplinary approach to assessment and intervention for children following a brain injury, but the definition provides specific areas for assessment procedures to address. A quick examination of this list of abilities reveals more assessment areas than are measured in a typical psychoeducational assessment.

Further, what is important about this definition is that it is, quite frankly, part of our special education law. This provides increased opportunities for children and adolescents who have sustained a brain injury to receive assessment and intervention services as long as there is disruption to learning in the school setting. This means that children and families now have legal rights within the educational system to pursue services in the event that concerns are not already being raised by school-based personnel.

The user friendly nature of these various definitions not withstanding, a myriad of issues remain that are critical to understanding a childhood brain injury. Noteworthy among these are: altered state of consciousness and severity, the presence of post-traumatic amnesia, and the presence of physical damage in the brain.

Table 1.1 Items and Categories on the Glasgow Coma Scale

Eye Opening	Best Verbal Response	Best Motor Response
4 - Spontaneous	5 - Oriented	6 - Responds to verbal commands
3 - Nonspecific reaction to speech	4 - Confusion, disorientation	5 - Localized movement to terminate painful stimulus
2 - Response to painful stimulus	3 - No sustained or coherent conversation	4 - Withdrawal from painful stimulus
1 - No response	2 - No recognizable words	3 - Decorticate posture
	1 - No response	2 - Decerebrate posture
		1 - No response

Altered State of Consciousness

As noted in many of the definitions cited above, something needs to be different following a brain injury. Indeed, one's conscious state is one of those things that can be different. Alterations in consciousness can be seen across the severity spectrum and tend to be a common feature of most brain injuries; however, a loss of consciousness is not a necessary component for a brain injury to have occurred.

For instance, a loss of consciousness may not be seen in selected types of focal injuries, concussions, or it may be delayed secondary to brain swelling (i.e., edema) or bleeding (i.e., hematoma). From an assessment perspective, this is an important feature for inquiry, but care should be taken when making a direct linkage between the presence/absence of an altered state of consciousness and a resultant brain injury (Jennett, 1986).

When an altered state of consciousness is suspected, there are several measurement tools available to determine the degree of the altered state. One tool, the Glasgow Coma Scale (GCS; Teasdale & Jennett, 1974) has been in use for nearly 40 years. It provides a simple index by which to determine the degree of altered consciousness and the severity of injury. The GCS is a clinical rating scale, typically completed by nurses, physicians, or other medical staff. It is designed to evaluate three key aspects of consciousness:

1. amount of stimulation to create an eye opening
2. best verbal response, and
3. best motor response.

Ratings range from a low score of 3 to a high score of 15. In general, a GCS score of

- ☐ 8 or less is indicative of a severe brain injury
- ☐ 9 through 12 reflect a moderate level of severity, and
- ☐ 13 and above indicate a relatively milder brain injury.

A score of 15 likely reflects the lack of an altered state of consciousness, but is very dependent on how long after the injury the GCS was completed. It is not typically completed at the exact time of injury as most individuals (e.g., Emergency Medical Service, First Responders) are not trained to administer the tool. In addition to providing some quantitative data on the degree of severity of a brain injury, it also has been linked to prognosis. Depth of coma has been significantly associated with mortality, while length of coma is a better predictor of outcome (Heiden, Small, Caton, Weiss, & Kurtze, 1983). Table 1.1 provides a description of the items and categories on the Glasgow Coma Scale.

Despite its wide-spread use with children and adolescents, Lieh-Lai et al. (1992) noted that there may be some limitations in predicting outcomes in children following a TBI. These investigators noted that in the absence of a hypoxic-ischemic injury, even the most severely injured children (i.e., GCS scores < 5) can recover a number of independent functions. Despite its various challenges (Lieh-Lai et al., 1992), the GCS continues to be used for individuals ranging from three years through adulthood; however, what is available for children younger than age three?

There have been a number of adaptations of the GCS specifically for very young children. Several of these include the Pediatric Coma Scale (Simpson & Reilly, 1982) and the Children's Coma Scale (Hahn et al., 1988). These scales follow the general configuration of the GCS, with the Children's Coma Scale substituting Best Behavior Response for Best Verbal Response. Most professionals who work with children with brain injuries rarely use these tools, as they tend to be administered most frequently by nurses. However, it is important for the evaluator to understand the nature of these scales and to look for them in the medical record as they provide important information as to the severity of the injury.

Degree of Post-Traumatic Amnesia (PTA)

This is a critical feature of traumatic brain injury as it provides another index of the severity of any injury; however, it also is one with which most professionals are not familiar. PTA, or anterograde amnesia, is the amount of time following a brain injury that an individual experiences difficulties learning and retaining new information. PTA is the time following an injury when the individual is conscious and functioning (i.e., not in a coma or significantly altered state of consciousness) and capable of responding in a relatively reliable manner.

The period of PTA ends when the individual's continuous memories are restored (Rosen & Gerring, 1986). Although there may be significant retrograde amnesia as well (i.e., the lack of recall for events prior to the injury), PTA has been deemed more useful for defining the severity of a traumatic brain injury. Earlier work by Brooks (1983) noted that a PTA of at least one week or more has been related to poorer outcomes in adults, particularly in the cognitive and psychosocial domains. From an assessment perspective, this becomes an important measure to find in the medical records as it may provide some indication of not only the severity of the injury, but also what types of measures may be most useful for the evaluation.

There have been several efforts to quantify the degree of PTA. Russell (1971) described a PTA of:
- less than 5 minutes as very mild
- 5 minutes to 60 minutes as mild
- 1 to 24 hours as moderate
- 1 to 7 days as severe, and
- greater than 7 days as very severe.

Similarly, Levin, O'Donnell, and Grossman (1979) developed the Galveston Orientation and Amnesia Test (GOAT) to assist in this endeavor. The GOAT is a 10-item bedside test of orientation and continuous memory that is administered serially to document the return of memory functions. Ewing-Cobbs, Levin, Fletcher, Miner, and Eisenberg (1990) modified this for children to produce the Children's Orientation and Amnesia Test (COAT). The COAT can be administered to children ages 3 through 15.

The ability of these procedures to be administered serially is important. Individuals with severe PTA can still exhibit islands of memory. The ongoing nature of this testing will assist in developmental surveillance and identification of deficits that are present following an injury. As with the GCS, most professionals working in an outpatient or community-based setting (e.g., schools) likely will not be familiar with these types of procedures for measuring PTA; however, knowing what information these measures provide will be critical to understanding the nature of the injury prior to conducting a more expansive type of assessment.

Presence of Physical Damage

A third major component of traumatic brain injury is whether there is any physical damage to the brain tissue. This information typically is seen via a variety of brain imaging procedures including neurophysiological (e.g., electroencephalography), structural (Computerized Tomography, Magnetic Resonance Imaging), and functional (e.g., functional Magnetic Resonance Imaging, Spectroscopy).

Although a description of these procedures is beyond the scope of this volume (see Barkovich & Raybaud, 2012, for a review of pediatric neuroimaging techniques), suffice it to say that these imaging procedures provide different types of pictures of the brain or brain activity and can target abnormalities that are secondary to an injury.

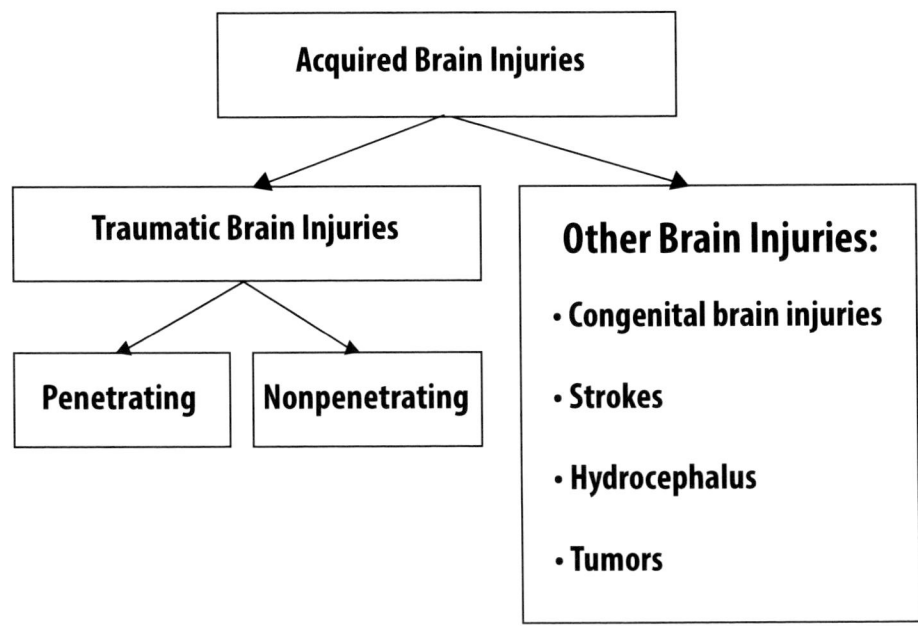

Figure 1.1 Different types of brain injuries

Additionally, it is important to note that absence of evidence of a brain injury on one of these procedures does not necessarily mean that an injury to the brain did not occur. This is typically the case in many less severe injuries (e.g., concussion); consequently, direct examination of functions, such as can be obtained from a neurological examination, neuropsychological examination, speech and language evaluation, and the like all can contribute evidence to the presence of a more subtle brain injury. Indeed, it also provides a strong argument for no brain or head injury to be taken lightly—even when there is no clear evidence of physical damage to the brain from sophisticated imaging procedures.

Findings from these procedures to document physical damage, when used jointly with the presence of PTA and the degree of altered consciousness, can offer a more comprehensive multidimensional approach to identifying a brain injury. Indeed, Levin et al. (2008) have demonstrated that children with mild brain injuries, and who showed documented brain pathology on Computed Tomography Scans (CT Scan) 24 hours after their injury, evidenced significantly poorer performance on the neuropsychological functions of working memory and visual-motor speed than those who did not show brain pathology.

Types of Brain Injuries

As can be seen by the definitions of traumatic brain injury and its associated core components, there are a number of issues specific to this diagnosis. What is important for the evaluator to understand, though, is that there are other types of brain injuries beyond ones that are "traumatic." This leads to the notion of acquired brain injuries (ABI) as a larger umbrella term to envelop all types of brain injuries that can manifest in childhood or adolescence.

As can be seen in Figure 1.1, and as noted earlier in the definitions offered by the Brain Injury Association of American, acquired brain injury allows for the inclusion of not only traumatic brain injury, but brain injuries that can occur from strokes, tumors, and other neurological events. Although the federal definition contained within IDEA has not changed to include an acquired brain injury model, a number of states have begun to examine this question with respect to how to serve these children and adolescents using assessment and intervention methods similar to those employed with traumatic brain injury.

Relatedly, there are also a wide variety of sequelae from brain injuries. These sequelae include:
- specific medical complications that can interfere with the assessment process, such as post-traumatic epilepsy and cerebral atrophy;
- physical features such as reduced stamina, hemiparesis, vision problems (e.g., field cuts, double vision), and headaches;
- neurocognitive challenges in nearly all areas of functioning;
- school and/or prevocational dysfunction (e.g., problems initiating and completing work, slow work pace);
- family problems; and
- social-behavioral difficulties (e.g., increased agitation).

In addition, variables such as age at the time of injury, premorbid functioning, and severity of the injury will contribute to the nature of subsequent immediate and long-term problems as well as the overall developmental trajectories of various functions.

The Special Condition of Concussion

It is important to note that a concussion is a traumatic brain injury that alters the way the brain functions. Effects from these relatively milder traumatic brain injuries are usually temporary however, in some instances they can be longer lasting and affect day-to-day functioning in ways that need to be understood in order to effectively facilitate the functioning of that child or adolescent. Although concussions usually are caused by a blow to the head, they can also occur when the head and upper body are violently shaken or via a whiplash type of force.

These injuries can cause a loss of consciousness, in many instances only for brief moments, but it also is important to note that one does not have to lose consciousness in order to sustain a concussion. In fact, upwards to 90% of concussions do not involve a loss of consciousness. Because of this, some people have concussions and they, and those around them simply don't realize it, although upwards to 170,000 children are treated in hospital emergency departments each year for a concussion (Colvin et al., 2012).

When a concussion or mild traumatic brain injury occurs, many of the **early physical symptoms include:**
- headaches
- blurred or double vision
- dizziness
- nausea
- vomiting
- agitation
- drowsiness
- seizures
- sensory sensitivity
- fatigue, and
- problems with balance and coordination.

Other symptoms can include **cognitive impairments:**
- problems with judgment and decision-making
- reduced attention
- sluggish processing speed
- diminished memory

There can also be **emotional symptoms:**
- irritability
- anxiety
- more volatility.

There can also be sleep difficulties (e.g., more or less sleep, trouble falling asleep), and complaints that they just don't "feel like themselves" (Lovell et al., 2004).

Taken together, these symptoms are referred to as ***Post Concussion Syndrome***. These symptoms tend to resolve in most individuals within 3-6 months (Babikian & Asarnow, 2009; Sroufe et al., 2010); however, some, such as headaches can remain for at least up to a year (Hooper et al., 2004). Unfortunately, many go undiagnosed and unrecognized!

Further, the notion of "absence of evidence (of brain injury) is not evidence of absence" is important here as even more sophisticated neuroimaging procedures typically do not find neurological damage. Needless to say, however, the multiple microscopic injuries that occur from a concussion can lead to significant neuropsychological and neurobehavioral impairments, with rates ranging from 15% to 35% (Babikian et al., 2011; Sroufe et al., 2010; Yeates et al., 1999) up to 12 months post injury. In one of the most comprehensive longitudinal studies of neurocognitive outcomes to date, Babikian et al. (2011) demonstrated the presence of deficits in memory, psychomotor speed, and receptive language abilities at 12 months following a well defined mild brain injury.

Interestingly, however, these findings were not specific to the pediatric TBI sample but, rather, reflected a general injury effect after controlling for age and parent education. Consequently, even in a relatively milder traumatic brain injury, the symptoms should not be ignored. Conversely, not all mild brain injuries will lead to long-term dysfunction, particularly if properly managed.

In the past, the severity of a concussion was reported in severity grades (i.e., Grade 1, Grade 2, Grade 3); however, contemporary clinical practice and associated nomenclature do not utilize this type of a system given the reliability and validity issues associated with such gradations in severity. The grading of the severity of a concussion was an attempt to link these relatively milder types of insult to the likelihood of an individual sustaining a permanent brain injury; however, of significant concern is the suspicion that even a subtle brain injury can have permanent consequences in a child's neurobehavioral functioning. In this regard, the idea of a "ding" to the head should always be taken seriously with respect to how it may affect a child's functioning over the short-term AND the long-term.

Another condition that can be associated with a concussion is **Second Impact Syndrome**. This can occur when an individual sustains a second concussion before symptoms from the first have resolved (McCrory, 1998). Acute brain swelling can occur when the second concussion is sustained and causes vascular congestion and increased intracranial pressure that may be difficult to control (Giza & Hovda, 2001). A second brain injury, or cumulative concussions, can be more dangerous than the first one and potentially life threatening. It also may take less of a blow to the head to cause a subsequent concussion AND it may take longer for the individual to recover. Further, given the developmental nature of brain growth, there is some suspicion that a child or adolescent actually may require more time to recover from a concussion than an adult; thus, making childhood concussions a significant health and school concern.

Although a concussion can occur from any type of blow to the head, there is a strong relationship of concussions to sports-related injuries. Recent data suggest that there is an estimated 300,000 sports-related concussions annually (McCrea et al., 2013). For anyone who even casually watches sports or reads a newspaper, these appear to be a daily event. Although a concussion can occur in any sport, they tend to occur more frequently in contact sports such as football, hockey, and soccer. Recent findings from a large sample of high school and college athletes (n = 570) indicated that only about 10% of athletes actually manifest symptoms and functional impairments beyond a 7 day recovery period following a sports-related concussion. The important nugget of information here, however, was that prolonged recovery tended to be related to indicators of more severe injury. These indicators included a period of unconsciousness, the presence of PTA, and the presence of elevated symptoms without deficits on cognitive or balance testing at 1.5 to 3 months post injury.

The strong relationship between the occurrence of concussions and sports has contributed to significant policy changes in how athletes are managed at all levels of play from preschool to professionals. Not only has the increased knowledge of this relationship contributed to policy changes of how medical management occurs on the field of play, examination of return-to-play guidelines, improvements in equipment, and public laws to govern high school sporting activities, it also has contributed to rule changes in how the game is played to lessen the chances of a brain injury (e.g., moving up the yardage line for kick-offs to lessen the violent collisions that typically occur on every kick-off return in football; penalizing helmet-to-helmet collisions in football; etc.).

Further efforts to protect middle school and high school athletes have also been made in many states by increasing the emphasis on conditioning and correct techniques to minimize the chances of a brain injury (e.g., tackling in football, heading the ball in soccer) (Mueller & Cantu, 2012; www.unc.edu/depts/nccsi), and by enacting youth sports concussion-related laws. In 2013, 47 states and the District of Columbia have enacted such laws. These laws typically address:
- ☐ brain injury education for coaches
- ☐ removal-from-play guidelines
- ☐ return-to-play guidelines including evaluation from an appropriate health care professional
- ☐ development of tracking mechanisms to monitor symptoms, and
- ☐ increase in awareness of concussions for parents and student athletes.

While these laws are notable and have advanced awareness of issues critical to brain injury and the athlete's health, it is important to note that none of these plans provide direct linkages back to the classroom setting via "return-to-learn" procedures, nor do any of the laws currently address youth sports below middle school. It is likely that amendments to these various laws will surface in the next several years to address the protection of our youngest athletes as well as to extend a formal reach into the school setting proper.

Finally, concussions pose an important consideration when considering how to assess and intervene with a particular student. How much assessment should occur? Who should do it? What procedures should be used? Although Chapter 13 provides some examples of assessment procedures that are being used for computerized assessment of cognition following a concussion, and the Post Concussion Checklist provides a vehicle for listing symptoms and their severity following a potential mild brain injury, the guidelines for appropriate assessment and management are only beginning to be asserted.

Further, with respect to return-to-learn issues, the specific classroom accommodations and/or services that may be most appropriate from one student to another can vary significantly. Should a student receive a 504 plan or should the student receive consideration for special education services? With more severe types of brain injury, of course, special education services may be a clearer pathway in terms of service provision.

The mild nature of most concussions excludes nearly all school-based special education services because most of these students won't show enough "serious concerns" or the presence of a disability even to receive consideration for a comprehensive school-based evaluation. Further, even if a student did receive a more thorough evaluation, the findings likely would not show major deficits; thus, placement for services under the classification of Traumatic Brain Injury likely would not occur.

But, depending on the time of year of the student's injury (e.g., spring), the slower processing speed, inattention, double vision, etc. may extend over multiple school years. This can take a serious toll on a child's learning, especially for high school students getting ready for college entrance exams, etc. In this regard, the special condition of concussion requires special consideration and monitoring to minimize the impact on school learning and general adaptive functioning for the student.

A Note on Screening for a Traumatic Brain Injury

Screening procedures to identify potential children and adolescents who have sustained a brain injury are clearly in their infancy. In general, formal screening should serve to identify individuals who have a problem or disability that warrants further attention or monitoring.

It is not designed to be diagnostic or prescriptive but, rather, to target children for some type of follow-up. Screening efforts typically employ brief, relatively inexpensive measures that can be quickly and easily administered by a variety of professionals and/or paraprofessionals. In addition, they should have good overall hit rates that increase the chances of identifying a child with a problem (i.e., TBI) and lessen the chances of making unnecessary referrals.

Consequently, rates of false positives (i.e., over referrals) and false negatives (i.e., under referrals) are needed in conjunction with good sensitivity (i.e., an accurate referral and subsequent identification of TBI) and specificity (i.e., an accurate non-referral or identification of a child without a TBI). With these broad guidelines for a satisfactory screening tool, suffice it to say that there are few, if any, such tools available to screen for TBI in children and adolescents at present; however, there remains significant need for a fine-tuned screening tool or method to identify children and adolescents who have sustained a TBI that has not yet been recognized.

There are several promising tools on the horizon, however, and these probably will become the first line of screening tools available for TBI in children and adolescents: the Screening Tool for the Identification of Acquired Brain Injury in School-Aged Children (STI; Dettmer, Daunhauer, Detmar-Hanna, & Sample, 2007) and the Brain Injury Screening Questionnaire (BISQ; Cantor et al., 2004). The STI is completed by parents and teachers of students in kindergarten through twelfth grade. The tool has four sections that include injury or illness; specific symptoms; behaviors that can interfere with school functioning and learning; and educational services that are being received. Initial reliability and validity for this tool was deemed satisfactory, although the specificity or the tool has not yet been determined. The BISQ is a longer tool that is completed by the student and there currently are costs required for training, scoring, and interpretation.

Other screening strategies, such as the Ohio State University TBI Identification Method (Corrigan & Bogner, 2007), are on the horizon, but they will require additional validation with school-age children. These screening tools have particular promise, but we will await the necessary psychometric data to support their use in widespread screening efforts in schools or other youth settings. In the meantime, examiners should be sure to include questions in their clinical histories and background forms pertaining to the occurrence of traumatic brain injuries.

Need for Comprehensive Assessments

Traumatic brain injury represents a significant public health concern. It has been estimated that traumatic brain injury represents one of the most frequent neurological conditions that results in the hospitalization of children and adolescents under 19 years of age. In fact, of all of the pediatric injuries in the United States, about 25% are related to brain injuries. Further, traumatic brain injury is the most frequent cause of death in children and adolescents with about a 41% rate of all child deaths. For those who survive, current prevalence rates for individuals, birth through age 25 years of age, range from 1.1 - 2.4 per 100 per year, a rate that is higher than previous studies have suggested (McKinlay, 2008).

In all age groups, boys are more likely than girls to have a traumatic brain injury, and blacks more likely than whites (Langlois, 2005; Langlois, Rutland-Brown, & Wald, 2006). Further, the impact of traumatic brain injury in fiscal terms has been estimated at more than $1 billion dollars per year (Schneier, Shields, Hostetler, Xiang, & Smith, 2006). Taken together, there are a significant number of children and adolescents who will require some form of assessment across hospital, school, and community-based settings. A comprehensive assessment actually may assist in lessening the fiscal demands of these injuries by better identifying specific needs and challenges and facilitating earlier intervention services (Catroppa & Anderson, 2009).

With the significant needs noted above, when does one make a referral for a comprehensive assessment? The answer is a simple and direct one—ALWAYS! Even in the instance of a concussion, the consideration of conducting a thorough assessment is absolutely essential in order to facilitate recovery and to minimize the chances that a second concussion could occur before the first one has resolved.

Conducted by a trained professional, a comprehensive assessment may assist in describing the cognitive sequelae that are suspected following a documented brain injury/insult and it may assist in determining the presence of a more subtle brain injury, especially when positive neurological findings are present. Most importantly, the true litmus test for many assessments is what it yields in terms of accurately documenting treatment needs and specific interventions. In this way, an assessment can facilitate discussion about what might be the best course of action for intervention for a particular child or adolescent following a traumatic brain injury.

In conjunction with the issues raised by the various definitions of traumatic brain injury, along with the types of brain injuries that can occur and its relatively high prevalence, there appears to be a strong need for more than just the IQ, achievement, and behavior rating scale triumvirate that tends to be the "bread and butter" of many psychologists. In fact, as we will see, this type of assessment runs the risk of missing a number of important cognitive functions by its relative lack of breadth. Indeed, traumatic brain injury is one of the leading health problems in our country, particularly for children. While recovery can and does occur, developmental trajectories and associated functions can be significantly altered.

This requires knowledge of traumatic brain injury mechanisms, the range of problems, and competency with a wide range of assessment strategies in order to identify ongoing issues and needs. However, much of this information typically is not taught in schools of education (e.g., school psychology programs), clinical psychology programs, or even rehabilitation programs. Many professionals who will work with a traumatic brain injury population have not been adequately trained to conduct the assessments or engage in treatment planning for these children. In fact, in one survey of school psychologists, the rates of endorsement of traumatic brain injury myths were not radically different than non-professionals (Hooper et al., 2006). The school psychologist's age, educational level, and years of experience did not affect their knowledge base in this specialty area, with about 85% of the school psychologists reporting that they needed more professional development to feel competent with this population (Hooper et al., 2006). As such, it becomes important for school psychologists and other professionals who will conduct evaluations of children and adolescents following a traumatic brain injury to increase their knowledge of and competence with this population.

Chapter 2
Types of Assessment

Numerous professionals can conduct assessments of children and adolescents following a traumatic brain injury. These professionals include, but are not limited to, nurses, clinical psychologists, school psychologists, neurologists, educational diagnosticians, pediatricians, speech and language pathologists, occupational and physical therapists, and a host of other professionals. In general, all these assessments are conducted to determine the:

- ☐ nature of a brain injury
- ☐ sequelae from the injury
- ☐ impact of the sequelae on school, prevocational, social, and family activities
- ☐ interventions that might be most effective at different time points in the recovery process, and
- ☐ tracking of recovery and response to various treatments.

Each of these professionals may be asked a different question that may demand a different type of assessment. It is important to ask the right question of the right professional in order to obtain a substantive answer.

Within the realm of pediatric traumatic brain injury and acquired brain injury, several major types of assessments tend to occur. These include the:

- ☐ neurological assessment
- ☐ psychological and psychoeducational assessment, and
- ☐ neuropsychological assessment.

Other types of assessments, such as speech and language, occupational therapy, physical therapy, and social work also are important. They typically are requested when specific problems with speech, language, motor difficulties, or family dysfunction are observed following an injury.

Neurological Assessment

All children and adolescents who sustain a traumatic brain injury will receive some type of medical evaluation, typically a neurological evaluation. The extent of the evaluation generally is dependent on the severity of the injury and where the child is being seen (e.g., pediatrician's office, emergency department, etc.). In general, the medical evaluation is useful in deciding the next steps in the treatment process, what other professionals need to be consulted, and/or whether more extensive neurodiagnostic procedures are required.

The neurological examination can vary from physician to physician, but several critical factors should be assessed in a neurological examination of the child or adolescent following a traumatic brain injury. One key factor is the state and quality of consciousness of the child, possibly including quantitative measures (e.g., the GCS). Another important factor relates to the importance of pupillary size and responsiveness to light. Over 20 years ago, Bruce and Zimmermann (1989) noted these features as being particularly important in recognizing abusive head trauma (aka shaken baby syndrome), and they remain core components of its identification today.

Here, it is important for the physician to conduct an examination of the optic fundi in order to diagnose retinal hemorrhages, which are common injuries associated with nearly all cases of violent shaking. In addition, the examination should focus on symmetry of spontaneous movements, station and gait, motor tone and strength in the extremities on both sides of the body, cranial nerve functions, sensory-perceptual functions, and the presence of various reflex responses. Measures of blood pressure, pulse, and respiration are also critical variables to be assessed during the initial neurological examination.

A mental status exam also can be informative where basic observations of affect, cognitive abilities, speech and language, memory, and fine-motor capabilities are assessed. When it is deemed necessary, more extensive neurodiagnostic procedures, such as electroencephalography, computerized tomography, magnetic resonance imaging, spectroscopy, etc. can be ordered so as to obtain detailed pictures of the brain and brain activity for examination (Menkes, Saral & Maria, 2005).

The neurological assessment is time efficient, typically being accomplished in less than 30 minutes in even the most thorough cases. These types of assessment provide significant information about the presence of major neurological problems, with a focus on lower level cerebral functions, although some higher-order cognitive processes are screened. In contrast, these procedures typically are not standardized, with each physician conducting the assessment in different ways and looking for somewhat different behaviors and functions. Consequently, the neurological assessment in many respects represents a good screening procedure to rule-out the presence of significant problems or concerns.

Psychological Assessment

Much like the neurological examination, the psychological assessment can take many different forms. In general, though, most psychological assessments are comprised of several major components. As mentioned in Chapter 1, these components comprise the triumvirate of intelligence, achievement skills, and social-behavioral functions. One major feature of the psychological assessment is that it tends to measure higher cognitive abilities.

> **Clinical neuropsychology is an applied science concerned with the behavioral expression of brain function/dysfunction. It is the study of the relationship between brain function and subsequent behavior.**

So, assessment of functions such as verbal reasoning, nonverbal problem solving, and psychomotor speed tend to be rather accurate. In addition, these procedures tend to be well normed and standardized such that findings can be compared across cases as well as across time points for a specific individual with good reliability and validity. In contrast, there is a cost for this degree of accuracy in terms of the increased time it takes to acquire these estimates. These types of assessments also rarely, if ever, include measures of lower cerebral functions. If these needs are present, then the involvement of other professionals (e.g., occupational therapist) can be useful.

Building a Neuropsychological Perspective – The Expanded Assessment

When the neurological examination and the psychological assessment are conceptually combined, the resulting product comprises both lower and higher level cerebral functions — this is what constitutes a neuropsychological evaluation.

Clinical neuropsychology is an applied science concerned with the behavioral expression of brain function/dysfunction. It is the study of the relationship between brain function and subsequent behavior.

The goals of a neuropsychological assessment include:
- ☐ Determining the presence of spared versus impaired abilities
- ☐ Understanding the impact of injury (e.g., TBI)
- ☐ Assisting in localization of function and dysfunction
- ☐ Assisting in determining whether to remediate or to compensate
- ☐ Generating (evidence-based) suggestions for remediation and compensation, and
- ☐ Monitoring and tracking progress across different settings.

Given the inclusion of both neurological and psychological features in a neuropsychological assessment, it becomes a critical consideration following a pediatric brain injury of any kind. The one stumbling block here, though, is that there are not enough trained pediatric neuropsychologists to address the large number of children and adolescents who may require these services each year. Further, with most of these children and adolescents remaining or returning to the school setting, it becomes paramount for other competently trained evaluators to employ a neuropsychological perspective in their efforts.

As noted above, the triumvirate of tests typically used in the psychological evaluation may not be sufficient for most children and adolescents following a brain injury, and the need for an expanded assessment becomes necessary.

While a measure of intelligence may be useful to target a general level of functioning, many of the intelligence tests provide little in the way of specific kinds of memory, receptive and expressive language, attention and executive function capabilities, or sensory-motor abilities. Complementing this triumvirate of tasks would provide a broader, yet more detailed description of cognitive abilities and, in turn, will yield a better profile of strengths and weaknesses following a brain injury. Subtle clusters of findings may be identified as well that could facilitate diagnosis in the event of a lack of findings on neurological examination and negative findings on neurodiagnostic procedures.

Additionally, the employment of such a perspective will enhance the data generated by an assessment and, hopefully, create other avenues for intervention in the community and school settings.

The neuropsychological perspective offers another vehicle for detailed tracking of cognitive recovery as well as ongoing developmental surveillance following a brain injury.

> **The neuropsychological perspective offers another vehicle for detailed tracking of cognitive recovery as well as ongoing developmental surveillance following a brain injury.**

Chapter 3
Neuropsychological Constructs and Expanded Assessment Procedures

Child neuropsychology has moved from being a relatively isolated area of interest to its own specific area within the field of neuropsychology. This advancement has been facilitated by the:
- increasing complexity presented by children referred for services
- improvements in medical science that have decreased mortality, but increased morbidity
- infusion of contributions by child development
- new measurement techniques of both brain structure and function, and
- improved training guidelines for the field.

There has been a steady evolution over the past 60-70 years, with neuropsychological assessment moving from an early beginning of using single tests to diagnose the presence of brain damage, to contemporary efforts steeped in trying to understanding the complexities inherent in a childhood brain injury.

Stages of Neuropsychological Assessment

Over 25 years ago, Tramontana and Hooper (1988) provided a chronology of the advances in neuropsychological assessment by describing different but overlapping stages in this history. These overlapping stages can be seen in Table 3.1.

Stage I

Termed the Single Test Approach, this stage lasted roughly from the mid-1940s to mid-1960s and had as its primary goal the global differentiation of children with brain damage from "normal." Primary features of this stage included the use of general, all-purpose measures of "organicity," with brain damage being conceptualized as a unitary construct. This approach produced a number of single tests for brain damage, such as the Bender Visual-Motor Gestalt Test (Bender, 1938), and tended to be strictly empirical and atheoretical in its application.

Table 3.1 Historical Stages of Neuropsychological Assessment

Stage	Approximate Time Frame	Goal
I - Single Test Approach	Mid-1940s to mid-1960s	Global differentiation of children with brain damage from normals.
II - Test Battery/Lesion Specification	Early 1960s to mid-1970s	Detection and differentiation of brain lesions.
III - Functional Analysis	1970s to 1980s	Specifying the behavioral effects of cerebral lesions; Identifying the underlying components of impaired performance.
IV - Ecological Analysis	Early 1980s to present	Relating assessment results to the child's everyday life and future potential; Specifying conditions for maximizing adaptive functioning.
V - Integrative Approach	Mid-1990s to present	A more precise integration of brain structures with corresponding brain function.

15

Stage II

The Test Battery/Lesion Specification Stage emerged in the early 1960s to mid-1970s. The primary feature of this stage was the use of a varied battery of tests (e.g., Halstead-Reitan Battery). The use of a battery of tests followed the greater appreciation for the variability of brain damage; however, there continued to be a strong emphasis on maximizing hit-rates in categorical diagnosis (e.g., brain damaged versus not brain damaged).

Stage III

Deemed the Functional Analysis Stage, it dominated the neuropsychological landscape from the 1970s to 1980s. During this time, the primary goals were to specify the behavioral effects of cerebral lesions and identify the underlying components of impaired performance. There was a de-emphasis on the use of neuropsychological tests to make inferences regarding brain lesions and, importantly, a "re-psychologizing" of neuropsychology where behavioral manifestations of injury began to take precedence. This stage saw an emphasis on neuropsychological description.

Stage IV

It was described as the Ecological Analysis Stage, with the activities during this stage surfacing from the early 1980s and extending into the present. According to Tramontana and Hooper (1988), the primary goals of this stage were to relate assessment results to the child's everyday life and future potential AND to specify the conditions necessary for maximizing adaptive functioning. Key features of this stage included the emphasis on neuropsychological prescription and evidence-based practice, evaluation of deficits relative to developmental and environmental demands, and utilization of a true biopsychosocial framework in interpreting neuropsychological results.

Stage V

Over the past 25 years since the Tramontana and Hooper (1988) anthology, a fifth stage has emerged, the Integrative Approach. This stage has proliferated since about the mid-1990s into the present, largely due to the rapid advancements in neuroimaging techniques, and nicely overlaps with Stage IV. The primary goal of this stage is to obtain more precise integration of brain structures with corresponding brain function. Here, there is use of more sophisticated neuroradiologic assessment procedures (fMRI, MRS) in conjunction with concomitant measurement of neurobehavioral functioning. This stage truly represents a 21st century merger of neurology and psychology, and should provide enormous clues as to the relationship between brain functioning and associated behaviors.

Approaches to Neuropsychological Assessment

Given the history of the evolution of child neuropsychological assessment, a number of major approaches to neuropsychological assessment have evolved. These include the:
- ☐ Boston Process Approach
- ☐ Qualitative Approach
- ☐ Fixed Battery Approach, and
- ☐ Eclectic Battery Approach.

Each of these approaches to assessment has relative benefits, but each one requires a strong knowledge base in brain anatomy and associated functions in order to interpret the data from a neuropsychological perspective. This is particularly important for children and adolescents with a brain injury and necessitates a firm understanding of various neurocognitive constructs being demonstrated.

Boston Process Approach

This approach to neuropsychological assessment was propagated by Dr. Edith Kaplan (Milberg, Hebben, & Kaplan, 2009) and requires the examiner to engage in hypothesis testing in order to determine what tasks to administer. In this approach, the examiner typically begins with a core battery of tasks, in most instances this core battery is based on an intelligence test. Based on the qualitative and quantitative findings that are manifested on this core battery, specific hypotheses are generated and additional satellite measures are selected to test these hypotheses.

Example:
An examiner may administer the Wechsler Intelligence Scale for Children-Fourth Edition (WISC-IV) and find that not only is the Perceptual Reasoning Index low, but the Block Design Subtest is particularly weak. The examiner could hypothesize that the child is experiencing visual-spatial deficits along with visual organization problems, and follow-up these hypotheses with measures assessing visual perceptual functions (e.g., Benton Line Discrimination, Benton Judgment of Line Orientation Test) as well as measures of executive functions (e.g., Delis-Kaplan Executive Function System).

Findings would support or refute the hypotheses proposed. Additionally, note that other areas of functioning, such as verbal abilities, processing speed, and working memory, did not receive any additional follow-up testing as it was assumed that these functions were intact and not necessarily disrupted by the injury.

The Boston Process Approach can be an enormous time saver with respect to testing time; however, it does require an astute examiner who is well versed in the quantitative and qualitative manifestations of injury, and knowledge as to how best structure the hypotheses to be tested so as to capture specific areas of impairment while at the same time not missing other areas of need because they were assumed to be intact. This approach also is dependent on the quality of the core measurement battery, not only in terms of its psychometric properties but also in terms of its breadth of coverage.

Qualitative Approach

This approach is perhaps one of the most challenging to master as it requires an extensive knowledge of brain functioning and how disease, damage, or dysfunction can affect these functions. Here, the examiner engages in significant behavioral observation of an individual so as to entertain various diagnostic formulations. In some instances, these observations are truly observations of behavior in selected settings and in other instances they constitute responses to a semi-structured interview or informal set of tasks to isolate specific neurocognitive abilities.

This approach was made popular by the famous Russian neuropsychologist, Alexander Luria, and it contributed to significant theorizing about various brain systems and functions well before neuroimaging procedures permitted a more detailed examination of the brain. Of the different approaches, this is one that will typically be employed in hospital settings and, quite frankly, it is the one that will require the most extensive knowledge base with respect to brain function and disease processes.

Fixed Battery Approach

This approach to neuropsychological assessment aims to provide a comprehensive assessment of brain functions using an invariant set of validated test procedures. This assessment approach typically is represented by the classic neuropsychological batteries, such as the Halstead-Reitan Neuropsychological Battery or the Luria-Nebraska Neuropsychological Battery-III, or by a fixed collection of separate tasks that are not modified in any way and used across all clients. Major emphases of this approach are placed on standardization and quantification, although the qualitative aspects of a child's performance also are considered in the interpretation of the results; however, the tasks and procedures do not change. Key advantages to this type of approach are that it serves to assure a consistently broad-based assessment, and it is replicable.

The latter advantage is important for TBI and other types of brain injuries in that multiple assessments likely will occur as the child moves through recovery or encounters new challenges in their surrounding ecology. In this way, it also provides a standard data base for comparative studies for both clinical and research endeavors. In contrast, the fixed battery approach generally does not provide an in-depth analysis of selected aspects of function—even if a specific area of asset or weakness is noted during the assessment and, by virtue of its namesake, it is inflexible.

The inflexibility is critical in that the fixed battery assumes a relatively high degree of patient compliance and it will be less accommodating to individuals with handicapping conditions that might interfere with task administration (i.e., the tests more than likely will not be administered). Of course, this does not preclude the examiner making observations and comments about brain functions; however, the battery of tasks may not facilitate these efforts under certain conditions.

The philosophical tenets of this approach also can clash with the need for sameness in the battery across clients and across time, and the frequent availability of revised tests and tools which will require changing the battery in the event that the decision is made to employ the most contemporary measures in the assessment process.

Flexible Battery Approach

When compared to the above three approaches, the Flexible Battery Approach is one of the most used approaches in the field of child neuropsychology. The approach combines the flexibility of the Boston Process and Qualitative approaches with the standardization and quantification of the Fixed Battery Approach. Here, there is at least an implicit outline of the relevant neuropsychological constructs that should be assessed. These constructs typically are theoretically and/or empirically driven and should provide sufficient breadth to cover most brain functions. Once these constructs are identified, any of a variety of validated tests may be selected to assess each functional area.

In general, psychometric properties and complementarity are usually key selection features. This selection process will preserve the quantitative aspects of the neuropsychological assessment and ensure a balanced and broad-based assessment if tests are selected according to key constructs. One key advantage over the Fixed Battery Approach is that it is adaptable to client or situational conditions, and it certainly is flexible with respect to upgrading to newly revised tools. This apparent advantage, however, will place possible constraints on replicability and comparability across clients and conditions, especially if the examiner is not thinking about the possibility of multiple assessments.

Further, problems may arise in making comparisons among measures that may differ in terms of norms, test construction, etc. This latter problem is critical to appreciate as there is a certain amount of error that is produced when multiple tests are compared across different normative groups. This is a common occurrence across different measurement approaches (e.g., Fixed Battery Approach) and, while test publishers have begun to address this issue by norming multiple tests on the same groups and statisticians can reduce this error by using sophisticated statistics, in the clinical realm this probably remains psychology's (and other disciplines engaged in testing) "dirty little secret," and typically has not addressed this potential measurement error.

Consequently, although the potential variable composition of a flexible battery may preclude validation studies on the battery as a whole, it is critical that the evaluator have a working knowledge of the validity of their measures and their content specificity.

Neuropsychological Construct Models

Brain-based research has contributed to increasing our understanding of the major functional domains inherent in both human and animal functioning. The four primary approaches to neuropsychological assessment operationalize these functions so that we can obtain a description of an individual's functioning following a brain insult or lesion, with each of the approaches describing a level and pattern of functioning across a number of different brain-based constructs.

To date, there are a variety of models that provide various neuropsychological constructs for measurement consideration. For example, from the Halstead-Reitan Neuropsychological Battery the constructs of tactile perception, visual perception, auditory perception/language, problem solving, and motor/psychomotor are extracted. Ewing-Cobbs and Fletcher (1987) provided six different constructs for consideration: language, visual-spatial and constructional, somatosensory, motor-sequential, memory and learning, and attention. Interestingly, Ewing-Cobbs and Fletcher suggested that, in addition to designing a neuropsychological battery around these core constructs, it is important to design the battery around what is known about the specific condition or disorder (i.e., if a disorder has a known deficit or asset, the battery should include measures to assess those features).

Construct models even have been explored for the preschool child (Wilson, 1992) wherein three major constructs have been suggested by conceptual and empirical efforts with associated subcomponents:
- language (auditory integration, auditory cognition, auditory short-term memory),
- visual (visual-spatial, visual cognition, visual short-term memory), and
- motor (fine-motor, graphomotor).

Although any of these construct models would suffice for the assessment of a child or adolescent following a brain injury, it is the theoretical model of Alexander Luria (1966) that has driven the development of many of our assessment approaches and the model that continues to be employed in a robust manner in contemporary neuropsychological assessment.

Lurian Neuropsychological Constructs

Lurian theory (Luria, 1980) has provided the field of neuropsychology with a robust amount of information pertaining to brain organization, functional systems within the brain, assessment of these functional systems, and strategies for management and rehabilitation. As part of his conceptualization of brain functions and associated measurement, Luria proposed seven major constructs for consideration. These included:
- motor
- sensory-perceptual
- attention
- language
- visual processing
- memory/learning, and
- intelligence.

The construct of intelligence was viewed differently by Luria than classic interpretations of intelligence in that he was referring to problem solving capabilities and abstract thinking, functions that have now been incorporated into the construct of executive functions. Taken together, each of the constructs was viewed as multidimensional as well as developmental in nature. When incorporated into the organization of a flexible battery approach, these constructs provide a broad-based assessment of brain functions and allow for the insertion of different types of formal and informal measures into the assessment process. In the following section, each of these functions will be described along with representative measures of each of the constructs.

SECTION II
Assessment Constructs and Procedures

Chapter 4
Motor Functions

Motor functions facilitate how we move around in our environment not only for sheer ambulation, but also enhance how we engage in recreational activities, manipulate objects with respect to dexterity and speed, and contribute to our general output capabilities. As can be seen in Table 4.1, there are a number of subcomponents of this large construct that will require consideration in the assessment process.

In addition to the major divisions between gross motor functions and fine-motor functions, there are a variety of other components of motor function including:

- ☐ simple fine-motor speed
- ☐ complex fine-motor speed generally involving some type of manipulation and dexterity
- ☐ motor coordination
- ☐ motor planning
- ☐ spatial-based movements, and
- ☐ balance.

Additionally, it is important to note that this domain of abilities also includes our oral-motor capabilities, which can be significantly affected if this system is damaged following a brain injury. Finally, it is critical to recognize that all motor functions have bilateral representation, and the motor functioning on both sides of the body need to be examined as part of a larger assessment of motor capabilities. When the motor system(s) is damaged or disrupted following a brain injury, the results can range widely from no problems or transient slowing, to the manifestation of different types of tremors, to hemiparesis and quadriplegia.

Findings in Children and Adolescents with Traumatic Brain Injuries

Specific motor deficits have been described for children and adolescents with traumatic brain injury. In more severe cases, a hemiparesis or quadraparesis may be evident in the gross motor system or significant motor balance issues may be observed. Often, however, children and adolescents show

Table 4.1 Representative subcomponents and measures within the motor construct

Motor Subcomponent	Representative Measures
Gross motor strength	Dynamometer
Basic fine motor speed	Finger Oscillation
Complex fine motor speed	Grooved Pegboard
Motor coordination and planning	Purdue Pegboard
Spatial based movement	Quick Neurological Screening Test-Revised
Oral motor	Dysphagia Evaluation Protocol
	Oral-Motor Feeding Rating Scale
Balance	Quick Neurological Screening Test-Revised
	Balance Error Scoring System
Lateral Dominance (Motor)	Edinburgh Handedness Inventory
	Harris Test of Lateral Dominance
	Reitan-Klove Lateral Dominance Examination

motor difficulties or slowing, perhaps more on one side of the body than the other. Many of these tend to improve or resolve over the process of recovery, typically within six months following the injury (Fuld & Fisher, 1977). Running speed and balance also can be disrupted (Chaplin Deitz, & Jaffe, 1993). Other types of motor deficits that have been reported, particularly in younger children, include problems with fine-motor coordination, difficulties with fine-motor integration, tremors, problems with rapid alternating movements (Dimitrijevic, Dimitrijevic, Kinalski, McKay, & Sherwood, 1987), and swallowing and motor speech difficulties (Morgan, Ward, & Murdoch, 2004; Ward, Green, & Morton, 2007).

Levin, Benton and Grossman (1982) also described motor slowing during the immediate time period following a mild, moderate, or severe head injury, although the severity of the injury was noted even at that time to exert a significant influence on the chronicity of the deficits. Findings in children with mild brain injury are mixed.

Gagnon, Forget, Sullivan, and Friedman (1998) found that their sample of children with mild brain injuries, ages 5 to 15 years, demonstrated significant differences from normative expectations on balance, response speed, and running speed and agility 13 to 18 days post insult. In contrast, Gulbrandsen (1984) reported that children with mild brain injuries did not differ from normal controls on simple motor speed tasks at 6 months post injury. For children sustaining a moderate or severe brain injury where cerebellar atrophy and other motor related brain structures are involved (Spanos et al., 2007), a number of motor impairments have been described. Specifically, investigators have reported deficits in simple and complex fine-motor speed, as well as in gross motor functions (Dumas & Carey, 2002; Kuhtz-Buschbeck et al., 2003), with these deficits continuing to be present at 1 year (Bawden, Knights, & Winogron, 1985; Chadwick et al., 1981; Winogron et al., (1984) and 2 year follow-up time points (Klonoff, Low & Clark, 1977). Further, available evidence also points to the vulnerability of motor functions in younger brain injured children wherein they demonstrated slower rates of growth in their motor abilities over a five year time span than children injured at an older age or children with less severe brain injuries (Thompson et al., 1994).

> **Further, available evidence also points to the vulnerability of motor functions in younger brain injured children wherein they demonstrated slower rates of growth in their motor abilities over a five year time span than children injured at an older age or children with less severe brain injuries (Thompson et al., 1994).**

Assessment Procedures

Historically, the assessment of motor functions has depended upon the procedures used in the neurological examination. Focal signs of motor dysfunction (e.g., hemiparesis, lateralized facial weakness) and problems with balance and gait typically have been conducted by physicians and other professionals with expertise in motor functioning (e.g., occupational and physical therapists). While not necessarily part of traditional psychoeducational or psychological assessments, the evaluation of motor functions typically is an integral part of a comprehensive neuropsychological assessment. In multidisciplinary or interdisciplinary settings, assessment of the motor functions can be facilitated by occupational therapists and physical therapists as part of their evaluations of motor function.

Most neuropsychological batteries include some measure of psychomotor speed, motor strength, and motor coordination. These types of assessments are useful in determining level and pattern of dysfunction. Additionally, it is important to examine asymmetry of performance. Children and adolescents should evidence a dominant hand advantage of about 10% to 20% on all motor tasks (Spreen & Gaddes, 1969).

Dominant hand advantages of less than 10%, or a nondominant hand advantage, are often suggestive of lateralized dysfunction in the dominant hemisphere. Conversely, a dominant hand advantage of greater than 20% may be indicative of residual deficits in the non-dominant hemisphere. In these instances, care should be taken to rule-out the presence of peripheral nerve injuries as these can impact motor strength, speed, and coordination as well.

Finally, in assessing motor functions, it is important that the examiner observe the child for qualitative signs of dysfunction. These can include associated movement or movements of extremities not involved with the motor task. Persistence of such extracurricular movements (e.g., when performing a task with one side of the body, overflow movements are observed on the other side) beyond age 10 often suggests dysfunction within the motor inhibitory system.

In addition to these assessment guidelines for measuring various motor functions, there are a variety of tests available that can assist in the assessment of motor abilities following a traumatic brain injury. These tests range from working with infants, toddlers, and preschoolers to those that are most appropriate for elementary, middle, and secondary students. As can be seen in Table 4.2, there are batteries of tasks that can be used for children and adolescents that assist in the assessment of motor functions.

Example:

The Peabody Developmental Motor Scales-Second Edition (PDMS-2) provides an assessment of both fine-motor and gross motor functioning in children ages birth though 5 years, and should prove useful for practitioners working with a preschool population. The PDMS-2 is comprised of six subtests that measure:
- reflexes
- stationary (body control and equilibrium)
- locomotion
- object manipulation
- grasping, and
- visual-motor integration.

Table 4.2 Representative Motor Batteries

Motor Batteries
Peabody Developmental Motor Scales-2
Bruininks-Oseretsky Test of Motor Proficiency-2
Bruininks-Oseretsky Brief Form
Bayley Scales of Infant Development-III Motor Scale Kit
Mullen Scales of Early Learning
Movement Assessment Battery for Children-2
Test of Gross Motor Development-2
Toddler and Infant Motor Evaluation (TIME)
The Infanib-Neuromotor Assessment of Infants
Miller Assessment of Preschoolers
Position and Fine-Motor Assessment of Infants
Dean-Woodcock Neuropsychological Sensory Motor Battery

These subtests combine to yield three major summary indices:
- Gross Motor Quotient
- Fine-Motor Quotient, and a
- Total Motor Quotient.

In addition to generating age-based standard scores, percentile, and age equivalents, the PDMS-2 also provides guidelines for making qualitative observations about a child's motor capabilities. Further, along with obtaining overall estimates of a child's fine-motor and gross motor abilities relative to a normed peer group, scores can be used to examine differences between specific motor functions as well as more generally between fine and gross motor functions. Taken together, this information can be used to develop treatment programs as well as to provide a quantitative means for tracking recovery of function.

Lastly, the PDMS-2 links obtained assessment findings to their Motor Activity Program. Although this program is not necessarily evidence-based, it does provide concrete suggestions for targeting specific goals, objectives, and associated intervention tasks that could be used in Individual Family Service Plan (IFSP) and Individual Education Plan (IEP) planning.

In addition to several motor batteries, such as the PDMS-2, there are a number of single test measures that permit examination of more focused skills and abilities following an injury. As can be seen in Table 4.1, one major example here is the Finger Oscillation Test from the larger Halstead-Reitan Neuropsychological Battery. This task requires the individual to tap with the index finger as quickly as possible for 10 seconds and the number of taps is recorded over 5 trials for each hand. This is a measure of pure fine-motor speed for each hand (with qualitative observations for coordination), and can be compared to normative standards for age-appropriate fine-motor performance. It also permits the examination of left hand-right hand differences in speed. This latter observation may provide one of the harder signs of a left or right hemisphere injury. Another task, the Grooved Pegboard allows for an examination of fine-motor speed, but also dexterity for each hand separately.

Yet another type of measure relates to balance, and provides important information pertaining to cerebellar injury. These types of measures are useful for different types of brain injuries, but have shown to be particularly important for determining the presence of a concussion. For example, the Balance Error Scoring System (BESS), part of the larger Sports Concussion Assessment Tool-2 (SCAT, 2009), is a measure designed to examine the quality of an individual's balance by assessing double leg stance, single leg stance, and tandem stance (i.e., heel-to-toe) across soft versus hard surfaces in a relatively quick amount of time. New technology also has begun to contribute to the assessment of balance as illustrated by the "Sway Balance" app. The Sway Balance is a forthcoming app designed to quickly assess an individual's balance, as one screening component of a concussion assessment, by asking the injured individual to hold the iPhone or iPad against their chest, close their eyes, and then perform the tasks from the BESS. Within minutes, a balance problem can be detected, particularly when compared to pre-injury levels.

Lateral Dominance and Handedness

Handedness is concept that describes a "preference" for one hand or the other in doing most motor tasks such as throwing a ball, writing with a pencil, or even reaching for an object. For most human beings, there tends to be a "dominant" hand, with the notion of handedness being present from birth. In orther words, this does not develop but, rather, becomes more clear with development. Most individuals are righted handed, with approximately 95% of people preferring to use their right hand for most motor tasks. In contrast, approximately 8%-15% of individuals prefer to use their left hand for most tasks.

A small number of people actually can use both hands equally well and are termed ambidextrous. Even these individuals may demonstrate a slight preference for one hand over the other for some tasks. The term mixed-handedness is reserved for people who perform different tasks better with specific hands. Finally, some people perform motor tasks equally poorly with both hands and are termed ambilevous or ambisinister.

Etiologically, there are a number of theories for handedness, but quite frankly, no one really has discovered a consistent reason. One line of empirical evidence (e.g., twin studies citing more left handedness in male twins) relates to the prenatal circulation of the neurotransmitter testosterone, with higher levels in the womb contributing to higher incidences of mixed and left handedness. A discussion of this evidence is beyond the scope of this text, but suffice it to say that the examiner should check for lateral dominance and related handedness patterns from a premorbid perspective as an individual can manifest many different handedness patterns following a traumatic brain injury.

A Cautionary Note

There are a variety of tasks provided in Tables 4.1 and 4.2; however, it is important to note that individuals can show motor problems that are not necessarily related to a brain injury. Individuals who have a peripheral nerve injury, such as might be seen with a ganglion cyst in the wrist, may show motor impairment on these tasks, but they are not central nervous system-based. In this regard, it becomes important for the evaluator to make sure that information is gathered as part of a motor assessment regarding medical history and pre-injury status prior to making any assumptions that motor impairments are a direct result of a brain injury.

Summary

Fine motor and gross motor abilities are fundamental to our functioning as human beings. When these functions are impaired, either permanently or in a transient manner, alternative coping mechanisms are essential, and a thorough assessment of these abilities is in order. This assessment should provide the foundation for understanding the impact of an injury on the motor system and associated adaptive capabilities, but also should lay the baseline for tracking change over the course of recovery.

Although a number of professionals can administer many of these assessment tools, working collaboratively with specialists in motor functioning, such as occupational therapists and physical therapists, should be a part of an interdisciplinary approach in children and adolescents with traumatic brain injury.

Chapter 5
Sensory Processing Functions

Description

Sensory processing functions refer to an individual's ability to sense, integrate, comprehend, and respond to information in the environmental (Miller & Lane, 2000).

Despite the available findings related to neurocognitive and neurobehavioral functioning following a brain injury in both children and adults, there have been relatively few studies that have examined the integrity of sensory processing functions following a traumatic brain injury. The few studies that do exist indicate the presence of sensory impairments following a childhood brain injury in nearly all sensory domains (Galvin, Elspeth, & Imms, 2009). These emergent findings clearly point to the importance of including an appraisal of sensory processing functions in an assessment of a child following a traumatic brain injury. Examination of sensory functions can yield important diagnostic information not only about the neurological basis of a brain injury, but also about the functional residuals.

From elementary human biology, there are five core sensory functions:
- ☐ taste
- ☐ smell
- ☐ touch
- ☐ vision, and
- ☐ hearing.

> **These emergent findings clearly point to the importance of including an appraisal of sensory processing functions in an assessment of a child following a traumatic brain injury.**

Any one of these sensory functions can be disrupted following a brain injury. The sensation component of hearing and vision typically is tested by a trained audiologist and vision expert (e.g., ophthalmologist, optometrist), respectively. There are also linkages to higher-order cognitive abilities in the form of language and visual-perceptual functions. In this regard, it is important that the evaluator recognize the importance of knowing the status of an individual's basic vision and hearing following a brain injury, and what impact any deficits may have on subsequent testing. This is a requirement of the special education guidelines and, quite frankly, common sense when any type of assessment strategy is implemented.

In comparison to the senses of vision, hearing, and tactile sensation and perception, the senses of taste and smell do not take as prominent a role when one thinks of school functioning and learning. However, they too can provide information pertaining to a site of injury and when disrupted, can affect day-to-day functioning in significant ways. Additionally, as with motor functions, the visual and auditory sensory-perceptual functions also have a lateral dominance component wherein most individuals will manifest a preferred eye for visual tasks and a preferred ear for hearing selected types of information. Let's examine each of these sensory-perceptual functional systems in turn and some associated strategies for assessment.

Vision

Vision is a complex system that affects not only what we see and how clearly we see it, but it also contributes to higher-order cognitive abilities (see Chapter 8). For the evaluator, it is common sense that the child needs to be able to see clearly for most assessment procedures to be conducted. At its most simple level, this will require a valid visual acuity screening for both eyes. This is a procedure that can be conducted by the school nurse, or at a more sophisticated level, by the appropriate eye specialist.

Ocular Dominance

Most individuals will prefer to use one eye over the other when doing tasks. This preference, or ocular dominance or eye dominance, is similar to left and right handedness, but it is important to note that handedness and eyedness do not always align due to the nature of the neurological innervation of each of these systems. As with motor functioning, ocular dominance is important to recognize, although the clinical significance of this is tempered by the fact that about two-thirds of the population is right eyed and about one-third is left-eyed. Further, some individuals do not show a clear preference for either eye. In typical binocular vision, the preferred eye is the one that is used for precise positional information. This may be especially important to a sharpshooter or an athlete engaged in shooting darts, arrows, a rifle, or even shooting a basketball or hitting a baseball. Measures of eye dominance are quick, and typically involve observation of eye preference to looking at pictures or objects.

Visual Impairments

Following a brain injury, visual impairments other than acuity difficulties can occur. These impairments may produce oddities in visual perception that can significantly affect a child's day-to-day functioning. One common finding following a traumatic brain injury is light sensitivity. Here, the normal emittance of a kitchen light will feel extremely intense and, perhaps, painful, without dark glasses or turning the lights off. This can be seen following brain injuries of all severity levels, including mild concussions, and fortunately tends to resolve over time.

A second type of visual problem that can occur following a brain injury relates to coordinated eye movements. This type of problem can be manifested in the form of abnormal eye tracking (i.e., ocular pursuit), disrupted visual saccadic movements, poor accommodation or ability to focus, and difficulties with alignment of the eyes. Taken together, these difficulties can affect day-to-day activities such as reading or driving.

Another common visual problem is diplopia, or double vision, wherein an object may be displaced horizontally, vertically, diagonally, or in some combination, thus creating two images of the object. This condition results from an injury to the neuromusculature for the eyes or from injuries to the cranial nerves for the eyes (cranial nerves, III, IV, and VI). Typically, diplopia occurs in both eyes but, more rarely can occur in only one eye. Not only can diplopia contribute to headaches and cognitive fatigue, but it also can impair a child's balance, ambulation, and reading skills. Assessment of diplopia is rather straightforward as the individual will generally self-report this oddity in visual-perception. When reported, however, follow-up by the appropriate eye specialist should occur.

A fourth vision residual from a brain injury that often can go undetected is a visual field cut. The assessment of visual field cuts typically is conducted by an ophthalmogist or optometrist, but screening for field cuts can be conducted by a number of professionals. Having a basic understanding of visual field cuts is important as it will affect how that child interacts with his or her surroundings as well as how others may interact with that child.

Although it is beyond the scope of this text to discuss the neurological underpinnings of the visual system, it is important to know that the information enters the eye through the retina and travels to the

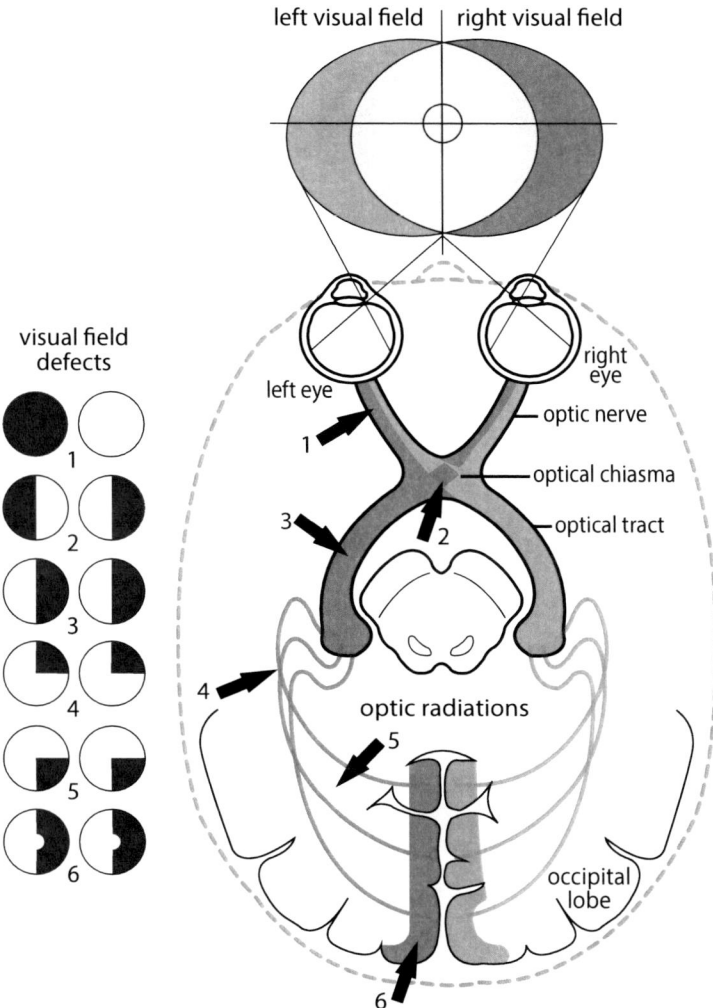

Figure 5.1. The visual pathway and examples of lesions leading to visual field defects

occipital region of the brain to the primary visual cortex via the optic nerve. Along the way, the optic nerve engages in a partial crossing of the pathway at the optic chiasma, with pathways through the temporal lobe on its way to the back of the brain. The partial crossing of the optic nerve at the optic chiasma contributes to the observation that about 50% of the visual information is processed in each occipital lobe. Consequently, the image that is represented in the retina of each eye can be divided in half, contributing to a left visual hemifield and a right visual hemifield, with each hemisphere contributing to the visual image that is perceived. This system is depicted in Figure 5.1. Assessment of the visual fields typically is conducted as part of most routine neurological examinations, but the fields also can be screened by a number of other professionals who are trained to assess the visual fields.

Specific damage to the visual pathway can create different types of visual field cuts. Importantly, from an assessment perspective, knowing the type of visual field cut can provide rather strong indicators of where the damage or disrutpion is in the visual pathway. As can be seen in Figure 5.1, disruption at location 1 is essentially the same as losing an eye as all vision is eliminated in the left eye. At location 2, the pathways to the nasal side of the retina are disrupted, so vision is lost from both peripheral sides of the each visual field. This is termed a hemianopsia. A lesion at location 3 on the visual pathway would yield a loss of vision in the right hemifield of both eyes. This is termed a homonymous hemianopsia.

As noted earlier, the visual pathways wind through the temporal and parietal lobes. A lesion at these junctures, as noted in Figure 5.1 at locations 4 and 5, would produce cuts in the visual quadrants. A lesion at location 4 would yield cuts in the upper right quandrant of the visual fields in each eye, whereas a lesion in location 5 would produce cuts in the lower right quandrant of the visual fields in each eye. Finally, with a lesion to the visual cortex at location 7, there is a clear hemianopsia in the right visual field; however, when the primary visual cortex is damaged, vision at the fovea is not disrupted, and a "notched" hemifield cut is noted.

Auditory

The auditory system, like the visual system, also is complex with necessary contributions to basic auditory sensation and perception and critical linkages to higher-order language-related functions (see Chapter 7). Unlike vision, however, the integrity of the auditory processing system is critical to language-related functions and overall communication. For the evaluator, it is common sense that the child needs to be able to hear clearly for most assessment procedures to be conducted. At its most simple level, this will require a valid auditory acuity screening for both ears. This is a procedure that can be conducted by the school nurse or speech and language pathologist, or at a more sophisticated level by a trained audiologist. Ear dominance is an important factor to consider in brain organization and how an individual may process auditory information following a brain injury, and there also are a number of auditory processing problems that can occur following a traumatic brain injury.

Ear Dominance

Like the motor and visual systems, the auditory system also has a contralateral organization in the brain, with damage to one side of the brain possibly causing difficulties in the opposite ear. Whereas the visual system is approximately 50% crossed, the auditory system is about 80% crossed; consequently, the concept of ear dominance is applicable. Given the different processing specializations of each hemisphere, along with the largely contralateral organization of this system, the concept of ear dominance is dependent on what specific auditory stimuli are being heard. In this regard, most people are right ear dominant for auditory-verbal stimuli. This is in large part because the left hemisphere is specialized for basic language-related functions. With the left hemisphere having about 80% of these fibers crossing over to the right ear, there tends to be a right ear dominance for language for most individuals. Conversely, for auditory non-verbal material, such as musical sounds or vocal tone and prosody, the left ear tends to be dominant. To determine such asymmetries, tests such as the Screening Test for Auditory Processing Disorders (SCAN) and the various professionally produced dichotic listening procedures can be most useful in the assessment process. Please see Table 5.1

Unlike vision, however, the integrity of the auditory processing system is critical to language-related functions and overall communication.

Given that the inner ear is wired directly into the central nervous system via the auditory nerve, hearing problems are not uncommon sequelae following a traumatic brain injury as both the organ (ear) and the central nervous sytem pathways can be disrupted.

Auditory Impairments

One of the major impairments that can manifest following a traumatic brain injury is a hearing problem. Given that the inner ear is wired directly into the central nervous system via the auditory nerve, hearing problems are not uncommon sequelae following a traumatic brain injury as both the organ (ear) and the central nervous sytem pathways can be disrupted. When the ear proper is damaged, the membranes of the inner ear and related structures (cochlea) are vulnerable to tearing and rupture. When the auditory nerve is involved, additional neurological complications will ensue. Taken together, these difficulties can result in children who have verbal and/or nonverbal auditory processing problems, conductive hearing loss (damage to the middle ear), or sensorineural hearing loss (damage to the inner ear or auditory pathways). Indeed, the rate of hearing impairment ranges from 16% to 32% for sensorineural and conductive hearing loss, respectively (Zimmerman, Ganzel, Windmill, Phillips, & Nazar, 1993). In addition to unilateral or bilateral hearing loss, associated problems can include:

- imbalance secondary to damage to the vestibular system
- vertigo
- tinnitus (ringing in the ear)
- hyperacusis (normal situations seem very loud)
- filtering background noise challenges, and
- auditory agnosia (i.e., sound/word recognition).

Unfortunately, many of these symptoms will linger following even a mild brain injury.

Table 5.1 Representative Batteries of Sensory-Perceptual Abilities

Sensory Domain	Representative Measures
Visual	ABC Ocular Dominance Test
	Miles Ocular Dominance Test
	Porta Test
	Tachistoscopic Examination
	Convergence Near-Point Test
	Visual Field Examination
Auditory	Dichotic Listening Tasks
	A Screening Test for Auditory Processing Disorders (SCAN)
Tactile	Graphasthesia Tasks
	Stereognosis
	Finger Localization Test
	Tactile Discrimination Test
	Two-Point Tactile Discrimination
	Sensory-Perceptual Examination
Smell	Scratch-and-Sniff Tests
	Olfactometer
Taste	Simple Taste Tests
	Electrogustometer

Table 5.2 Sensory Domains and Representative Measures

Sensory-Perceptual Batteries
Dean-Woodcock Neuropsychological Sensory Motor Battery
Sensory Profile
DeGang-Berk Test of Sensory Integration
Quick Neurological Screening Test-Revised

From an assessment perspective, the need for interdisciplinary team involvement is important. Following a traumatic brain injury, it is essential that all children and adolescents receive an otoscopic examination and audiologic screening to assess the integrity of the hearing system; however, there is a strong sense that this is not the case, particularly for those sustaining milder injuries (Haarbauer-Krupa, 2012). The routine need for this is further accentuated by the observation that many individuals and their families will not recognize that they have a hearing problem. Questions pertaining to hearing problems and related auditory impairments should be a routine component of any post injury interview.

Tactile

As with motor functions, perhaps one of the most reliable diagnostic indicators of lateralized dysfunction or damage comes from left-right differences in tactile perception in the hands and face. For non-injured typically developing individuals, there should be few or no tactile perception errors when such challenges are applied. Following a brain injury, however, significant differences between the right and left side of the body can indicate where an injury occurred and/or what residuals may be present. Given the organization of the sensory-motor region on the central sulcus of the brain, dysfunction in tactile functions typically indicates damage or disruption to the contralateral hemisphere. As can be seen in Table 5.1, tactile kinesthetic functions are easy to examine with tasks that do not require a great deal of time. Tests such as graphasthesia (i.e., recognition of shapes, letters, or numbers drawn on the hands or fingertips), stereognosis (i.e., recognition of objects by touch), finger localization, and two-point tactile discrimination all can yield important information concerning tactile discrimination and tactile perception functions. Some of these tasks are listed in Table 5.1. Batteries of sensory functions that include tactile sensory and perception tasks also are available and are illustrated in Table 5.2.

As noted in Chapter 4 for interpreting motor signs, an interpretive caution should be asserted to the astute examiner for tactile processing findings. Although many tasks, such as fingertip number writing and stereognosis, tap tactile functions, they also can be influenced by other factors (e.g. attention or language). In this regard, it will be crucial for the examiner to conduct a thorough examination in order to determine if observed errors or inefficiencies are strictly due to tactile impairment, other factors, or a combination of difficulties. This may require the use of both formal and informal measures along with close observational skills on the part of the examiner.

Olfactory (Smell)

Simply speaking, the sense of smell is defined by the nose perceiving a specific odor. Nerve cells positioned in the nose are excited by environmental odors (e.g., a holiday dinner), and those cells then communicate with the olfactory nerve in the brain. Although our sense of smell as human beings represents one of our weakest senses, it also is one of the most susceptible to damage following a traumatic brain injury. One of the primary reasons for this is that the olfactory nerve is the only cranial nerve that does not originate in the brain stem. In fact, the olfactory bulbs (yes, there are two of them) are located in the region of the left and right frontal poles.

With a large number of brain injuries being related to damage to the prefrontal cortex, the olfactory bulbs are precariously vulnerable to damage as well given their location in the frontal regions. Current estimates suggest that approximately 1% to 2% of the population below the age of 65 has some type of smell impairment (National Institute of Deafness and Other Communication Disorders, 2012; www.nidci.nih.gov); however, there are precious few data on children and adolescents, and even fewer studies examining its prevalence in pediatric brain injuries. Further, these estimates are complicated by the fact that smell dysfunction can be comprehensive, partial, or odor specific.

> **Following a traumatic brain injury, it is essential that all children and adolescents receive an otoscopic examination and audiologic screening to assess the integrity of the hearing system; however, there is a strong sense that this is not the case, particularly for those sustaining milder injuries**
> (Haarbauer-Krupa, 2012).

Part of this challenge relates to the relatively infrequent assessment of smell functions following an injury. Given that smell disorders are relatively rare in children, there is a reasonable baseline in place in the event that a smell problem is identified following a traumatic brain injury. In one of the few studies examining smell functions in children following a brain injury, Sandford et al. (2006) revealed about an 8% rate of hyposmia, with greater severity of traumatic brain injury being associated with poorer olfactory abilities. These investigators noted the importance of conducting olfactory testing following a brain injury, with a particular emphasis on examining the integrity of the olfactory nerve.

Disorders of smell are difficult to diagnose and their appearance in children and adolescents are relatively rare. Subsequently, the assessment of smell functions typically is not routinely conducted. There are several validated tests for olfaction and, generally, they tend to be easy to administer, quick, and inexpensive. One strategy for screening for olfactory functions includes a series of bottles containing specific odorants (e.g., chocolate). Here, the individual is asked to block one nostril and smell the contents of the bottle with the other. Once one nostril has been checked, the second nostril is screened. This assessment should provide an estimate of the person's smell capabilities and also provide information related to whether one or both olfactory pathways has been injured. A similar set of procedures are illustrated by the University of Pennsylvania Smell Identification Test (UPSIT) wherein a "scratch-and-sniff" version of the bottles has been created; the Brief Smell Identification Test, Odor Stick Identification Test, the Sniffin Sticks Test, the Scandinavian Odor Identification Test, and the Smell Diskettes Test.

In addition to olfactory identification, there are a number of tasks that attempt to assess smell threshold. For example, the Connecticut Threshold Test, the Sniffin Sticks Threshold Test, the European Test of Olfactory Capabilities, and the Smell Threshold Test. For each of these tasks, the assessment strategy is to determine the weakest concentration of a specific smell e.g., n-butanol, phenyl-ethyl alcohol) that the individual can detect. Scoring of these procedures allows for determination of the severity of hyposmia as well as determination of a total lack of smell sensation (i.e., anosmia). Olfactometers also are being used more frequently and provide a precise estimate of the laterality of smell; however, their use continues to be largely within the research realm.

Generally speaking, these are not tasks on which most professionals, medical or non-medical, have been trained. In that regard, the interdisciplinary approach is important where referral to an otolaryngologist (i.e., ear, nose, throat specialist) might be most useful once any screening is completed following a traumatic brain injury.

Gustatory (Taste)

Our sense of taste is probably one of the more enjoyable aspects to our array of sensory capabilities. For anyone who enjoys good food, this certainly is the case. At its most basic level, taste is defined as the perception of five sensations by the tongue: salty, sweet, sour, bitter, and umami (savory). The taste of metal also has been suggested, along with several other sensations (e.g., astringent, electric), but these remain ongoing scientific debates. The tongue is the critical organ in this process. The tongue has many, many taste buds, and associated receptors for the five basic tastes are scattered across all regions of the tongue to some degree.

> **Although our sense of smell as human beings represents one of our weakest senses, it also is one of the most susceptible to damage following a traumatic brain injury.**

Neurologically, the sense of taste is orchestrated by three cranial nerves: the facial (VII), glossopharyngeal (IX), and vagus (X). The glossopharyngeal nerve is the primary contributor to the sensory experiences of the tongue, while the facial nerve facilitates taste sensations from the anterior two-thirds of the tongue. The vagal nerve is responsible for providing the neurological connections to the taste buds located at other regions in the oral peripheral region. Given the activity of these cranial nerves in the sense of taste, any injury to the brain stem or to the cranial nerve connections arising out of the brain stem could lead to a disruption of the sense of taste.

Interestingly, there also can be ipsilateral or bilateral impairment of the taste mechanism, as well as disruption of different types of tastes, depending on the nature of the brain injury. These disruptions can lead to a total loss of taste (*ageusia*), diminished taste (*hypogeusia*), or specific types of disordered tastes (e.g., *dysgeusia*). The manifestation of pure taste disorders is relatively rare, so if a child or adolescent is complaining of a disruption in taste functions following a brain injury, then an evaluation of the taste mechanism should be pursued.

The assessment of the sense of taste is challenging, and sometimes it is hard to separate from the assessment of smell. Indeed, after a brain injury, individuals often complain of taste problems when, in fact, they more likely have an olfactory problem. To assess for a taste disorder, a taste test can be conducted (Table 5.1). Here, liquids that represent the various tastes (e.g., sweet, sour) are given to the individual and they are simply asked to identify the taste. An added condition strengthens or weakens the concentration of the specific tastant in an effort to determine the lowest threshold for identifying that taste. This type of procedure is deceptively simple in that interpretation is highly subjective, and there are few opportunities to determine whether there is a problem with taste quality or taste intensity. There also is the challenge of attempting to localize the taste disruption, by testing both left and right sides of the tongue, in an effort to identify which cranial nerve was affected.

Finally, it is important to note that nearly all of this research has been conducted with adult survivors, and little empirical evidence exists for children. In this regard, several efforts have been asserted to standardize the assessment of taste by using electrogustometers (Table 5.1). The electrogustometer produces a weak electric current on the tongue to stimulate a sour taste. Although these types of procedures appear reliable (Berling et al., 2011), there is little to no work with children, and a dearth of studies of individuals post traumatic brain injury more generally. As with the sense of smell, working with a team of individuals to assist in this assessment will be critical.

Summary

As can be seen in Tables 5.1 and 5.2, there are a number of tasks that are available to assess the sensory functions in a child or adolescent following a traumatic brain injury. Although many of these tasks may be familiar to a neuropsychologist or other medically-based professionals, it is equally likely that a number of these measures will seem foreign to examiners conducting assessments in the school or community setting. To further compound the lack of familiarity of professionals with a number of these procedures, there are not a large number of studies examining sensory-perceptual abilities in children and adolescents following a brain injury. This is especially true for the senses of smell and taste. Nonetheless, for professionals working with children following a traumatic brain injury, it will be essential to have some indication of the integrity of these systems as they provide the building blocks for higher cognitive abilities. If these systems are impaired, it is highly likely that higher-order cognitive processes will be affected. This will be especially important for the very young child who sustained a traumatic brain injury as this child's learning is only beginning, and the sensory perceptual building blocks will be disrupted. Lastly, it is important for professionals working with a pediatric traumatic brain injury population to work collaboratively across disciplines such that a thorough evaluation of all sensory functions is conducted.

> **At its most basic level, taste is defined as the perception of five sensations by the tongue: salty, sweet, sour, bitter, and umami (savory).**

Chapter 6
Attention Functions

Description

Despite our day-to-day use of the term, "attention" is not a unitary construct. In actuality, attention processes are multidimensional and embedded within a developmental framework. To date, there are numerous models of attention, such as those proposed by Mirsky et al. (1991), Posner and Peterson (1990), and Barkley (1997), and those that have evolved from children with TBI (e.g., Park, Allen, Barney, Ringdahl, & Mayfield, 2009). All of these models are multidimensional and they have strong linkages to neurological underpinnings that mediate the various processes of attention. These models also have contributed to the evolution of evidence-based attention intervention programs (e.g., Sohlberg & Mateer, 2001; Stierwalt & Murray, 2002) and associated attention training clinical guidelines (Sohlberg et al., 2003). Despite the various differences and nuances of each of these attention models, most models of attention include some aspects of the following subcomponents:

- ☐ focused or selective attention
- ☐ sustained attention
- ☐ divided attention, and
- ☐ alternating or shifting attention.

Selective attention

The subcomponent of selective attention pertains to how well an individual can focus on the specific details of an object or task, while at the same time paying less attention to surrounding details that are not relevant to the task at hand (i.e., not being distracted by everything else that is going on in one's surroundings). Children who have difficulty with this component of attention tend to be distractible and, at times, disconnected in their actions and behaviors.

> **Focused attention pertains to the individual's awareness to sensory stimuli in their environment.**

The most basic level of selective attention is focused attention. Focused attention pertains to the individual's awareness to sensory stimuli in their environment. This level of attention is typically disrupted when altered consciousness is experienced following an injury, such as when low overall arousal levels are present or when an individual is coming out of a coma.

Sustained Attention

The duration that an individual can maintain their focus is called *sustained attention*. This subcomponent of attention also refers to vigilance, or "stick-to-it-ness." Children with difficulties in this subcomponent will have performance inconsistencies, cognitive fatigue, and frequent attention slippages during various tasks.

Divided attention

This is the ability to share attention while performing two or more tasks of equal importance. This is not necessarily the same as being able to "walk and chew gum at the same time," as the tasks have to be of somewhat equal importance, but this type of attention probably is more ecologically valid with respect to day-to-day occurrences as most people are typically multi-tasking in some fashion.

Alternating attention

Finally, the alternating or shifting of attention pertains to how an individual can move from one task to another with minimal disruption. Impairment in this attention subcomponent can manifest in the form of:

- ☐ perseverative thoughts or behaviors
- ☐ cognitive rigidity, and
- ☐ significant difficulties with transitions.

The divided attention and alternating attention subcomponents also have strong linkages to executive functions, and these will be reviewed in Chapter 10. Although empirical data examining these specific subcomponents of attention in pediatric traumatic brain injuries have only begun to surface (Park et al., 2009), they do hold potential for better understanding the impact of a traumatic brain injury on attentional functions and regulation.

Findings in Children and Adolescents with Traumatic Brain Injury

One of the most common findings in pediatric traumatic brain injury is the presence of various types of attention problems (Hooper et al., 2004; Stierwalt & Murray, 2002). This is largely the result of the vulnerability to injury of the neurological systems that mediate attention in the brain stem, prefrontal cortex, and right hemisphere (Wilde et al., 2005). These types of problems have been reported across the age span as well as injury severity, with younger (Catroppa & Anderson, 2003; Van Heugten et al., 2006) and/or more severely injured (Yeates et al., 2005) children showing greater impairments in attention. Attention dysfunction is particularly obvious during the acute phases of injury, even in mild traumatic brain injury, and one of the reasons why the assessment of attention for any type of brain injury is necessary.

Despite the frequent finding of attention problems in children and adolescents following a traumatic brain injury, the state of the literature is less than clear. Part of this challenge lies in the fact that attention is defined in a number of ways, or not defined, and various measures are used. Further, some of the attention measures are confounded by the fact that other cognitive functions (e.g., motor speed) are required to complete the task and a direct linkage to attention is not possible. Despite this state of the field, a number of specific findings related to attention have surfaced.

Children with severe traumatic brain injury have been shown to exhibit deficits in selective attention at least one year post injury (Catroppa & Anderson, 2005); however, these type of deficits were not different from a mildly injured comparison group at two (Catroppa & Anderson, 2005), five (Catroppa et al., 2006; Ewing-Cobbs et al., 1998), and six years after the injury (Anderson et al., 1998). A similar pattern of findings has been documented within the subcomponent of sustained attention where initial deficits are present (Catroppa & Anderson, 2005), but then resolve by at least one year post injury (Wassenberg, Max, Lindgren, & Schatz, 2004).

Using more complex measures though, sustained attention impediments have been documented at least five years post injury when compared to mildly impaired groups (Catroppa et al., 2006). Deficits in both divided attention (Anderson et al., 1998) and attention shifting (Park et al., 2009; Van Heugten et al., 2006) have been reported in children with severe traumatic brain injury, although the persistence of these deficits over time remains unclear. Specifically, Anderson et al. (1998) have shown long-standing deficits in divided attention about six years post injury, but the impairments of attentional shifting seem to improve over at least a five year period following the injury (Ewing-Cobbs et al., 1998; Van Heugten et al., 2006).

Relatedly, deficits in concentration and speeded performance have been documented up through one year post injury, and these findings seem to hold for individuals sustaining injuries at all levels of severity (Bawden et al., 1985; Winogron et al., 1984).

Closely related to the symptoms of attention disruption following a brain injury, is the diagnosis of Attention Deficit Hyperactivity Disorder (ADHD). Although children with ADHD are more likely to sustain a brain injury secondary to their heightened impulsivity and inattention (Hamock & Mayfield, 2005), the prevalence of children meeting ADHD criteria who have sustained a brain injury

> **Attention dysfunction is particularly obvious during the acute phases of injury, even in mild traumatic brain injury, and one of the reasons why the assessment of attention for any type of brain injury.**

is approximately 20% (Yeates et al., 2005) to 50% (Armstrong et al., 2005). Indeed, hyperactivity and poor attention have been reported by parents at follow-up intervals, with some results suggesting that these deficits can persist for up to five years post injury (Klonoff et al., 1977). To reiterate the principle above, however, from an assessment perspective it will be important to disaggregate the notion of attention as a multidimensional cognitive process from attention as a disorder (i.e., ADHD).

Understanding these profiles of attention will be critical to characterizing the attention residuals following a traumatic brain injury. Moreover, it is important at this point to make a clear distinction between understanding attention as a multidimensional cognitive process versus attention as disorder. The former permits the study of attention as it relates to cognitive functioning. In this regard, utilizing the multidimensional components as described above, or another cognitively-based model of attention will be in order. In contrast, understanding attention as a disorder invokes the notion of Attention Deficit Hyperactivity Disorder (ADHD), and implies the use of behavioral mechanisms for defining the condition (APA, 2013).

While it is expected that some aspects of attention likely will be disrupted in ADHD, the assessment process for ADHD is clear (American Academy of Pediatrics, 2011) and does not necessarily require a formal assessment of attention subcomponents to arrive at a clinical diagnosis. Further, as you will see, the relationship between ADHD and traumatic brain injury is noteworthy, but separating out attention as a process versus attention as a disorder will facilitate the evaluation process.

> Although children with ADHD are more likely to sustain a brain injury secondary to their heightened impulsivity and inattention (Hamock & Mayfield, 2005), the prevalence of children meeting ADHD criteria who have sustained a brain injury is approximately 20% (Yeates et al., 2005) to 50% (Armstrong et al., 2005).

Assessment Procedures

There are precious few attention batteries that have been developed to date that focus on the various subcomponents of attention and their developmental constraints across the ages. For example, the Test of Every Day Attention for Children (TEA-CH; Manly, Robertson, Anderson, & Nimmo, 1998) provides one of the few comprehensive measures that targets selective attention, sustained attention, divided attention, attention shifting, and inhibitory control of both verbal and motor responses for children and adolescents ages 6 to 15 years. In contrast, the field has a number of single measures designed to assess the subcomponents of attention (See Table 6.1). It is important to note that many of these tasks have the potential to measure multiple subcomponents of attention, but a number of these tasks will be confounded by the influence of other cognitive functions (e.g., memory, motor speed, etc.). The astute examiner will be vigilant with respect to the limitations of the measures and the multiple interpretations that can be present.

Within the selective attention subcomponent, measures such as the Halstead-Reitan Trail-Making Test and the various cancellation tasks (e.g., letters, numbers, objects) have been employed. Timed discrimination tasks for verbal and nonverbal stimuli also have been used to assess selective attention. In general, these measures require the individual to focus on or locate selected items, and typically have a timed component to highlight their efficiency.

For sustained attention, a wide variety of continuous performance tests (CPT) are available, with each of the CPTs following a specific attention paradigm requiring a certain amount of time and perhaps extending across different modalities.

Example:

The Gordon Diagnostic System (GDS) requires the individual to push a button as quickly as they can when they see the number 1 followed by the number 9. In contrast, the Conners Continuous Performance Test (CPT-II) presents similar stimuli, but requires the individual to constantly push the mouse button until they see the targeted combination. Several of these tasks have both visual and auditory components, allowing for measurement across modalities, with time spans for the various tasks ranging from 9 minutes (GDS) to 22 minutes (Test of Variables of Attention) for the standardized versions. If normative data are not critical, then many of the CPT tasks can be programmed to be shorter. Although there likely will be no normative data to assist in interpretation, these modifications may prove useful in getting an initial assessment and then tracking a child's progress as they move through recovery.

The measurement of shifting attentional set crosses over into the measurement of various executive functions and will be mentioned in Chapter 10. Much less work has been conducted with assessing divided attention in pediatric traumatic brain injury, but there are a variety of dual-task paradigms that are available in the experimental literature.

A representative listing of attention measures by subcomponent is provided in Table 6.1.

Summary

Given that attention impairments can be seen across the range of severity in children and adolescents with traumatic brain injury, the assessment of attention should be a critical aspect of a childhood evaluation following a brain injury. As such, it is important for the examiner to consider the multidimensional aspects of attention and how the selected measures may contribute to each of the subcomponents. Additionally, it is important for the examiner to remember the limitations of these measures as they may be compromised by the interference of other cognitive dysfunctions. Lastly, while ADHD is an important consideration for children who have sustained a traumatic brain injury, particularly given the relationship of traumatic brain injury to ADHD and the potential for stimulant medications to assist in treatment when warranted, keeping the notion of attention as a multidimensional cognitive process versus attention as a disruptive behavior disorder separated will be important in attempting to understand the cognitive residuals following a traumatic brain injury.

Table 6.1 Subcomponents of Attention and Representative Measures.

Attention Subcomponent	Representative Measures
Selective Attention	Trail-Making Test
	Cancellation Tasks (Numbers, Letters, Objects)
	Speeded Discrimination Tasks
Sustained Attention	Gordon Diagnostic System
	Conners Continuous Performance Test
	Test of Variables of Attention
	Intermediate Auditory and Visual CPT
	Vigil
Divided Attention	Dual-Task Paradigm Tests
Attention Shifting	Wisconsin Card Sorting Test
	Contingency Naming Test
	Stroop Color and Word Test

Chapter 7
Language Functions

Description

Language capabilities arguably are some of the most critical functions that make us human beings. Language abilities are critical to basic interactions with other people, not only for simple communication but also for social interaction. They are essential to much of our learning. Language is a complex set of systems that not only require multiple brain regions, but also may be organized somewhat differently in the brains of males versus females. Linked intimately to our auditory processing functions (see Chapter 5), language abilities tend to have a relatively slower, but longer developmental trajectory than many other higher-order cognitive abilities. For example, our growth of vocabulary words begins early and increases to nearly 3,000 words by the time most children reach elementary school; however, this is a function that will continue to grow every day, with growth extending into geriatric years if one remains modestly active with reading and other verbal activities. A traumatic brain injury at any point along this developmental trajectory will place the language functions that are in active ontogeny at great risk for delay and/or disruption.

Further, language abilities have a long history of being compartmentalized in terms of their understanding. Although specific language functions have been aligned with specific regions of the brain, it is important to note that this compartmentalization of various language functions does not imply total independence as there is significant interaction between them. With that said, a working knowledge of the basic types of language functions is in order and includes the core subcomponents of expressive, receptive, and pragmatic abilities.

Expressive Language

Expressive language relates to how we express ourselves to others. It even relates to how we engage in private self-talk. Like many cognitive abilities, expressive language is complex and multidimensional.

> **A traumatic brain injury at any point along this developmental trajectory will place the language functions that are in active ontogeny at great risk for delay and/or disruption.**

First and foremost from an assessment perspective, it is important to take into account an individual's communicative intent. This is a concept that applies to infants without their first expressive utterances as well as to individuals with well developed vocabularies. The basic question for most evaluators is, "Does this individual want to communicate?" The lack of willingness to communicate, or a lack of interest in communicating can be associated with a variety of reasons, including a brain injury. It is important that the evaluator obtain an immediate assessment of communicative intent as it will facilitate the rest of the evaluation.

Once integrity of the communicative intent is determined, a variety of other expressive language capabilities should be evaluated either formally or informally.

- ☐ Can the individual engage in naming tasks or is there evidence of circumlocutionary behavior where the person is trying to find the word but is talking all around it?

- How intact is word and phrase repetition?
- What is the organization of the general verbal output? Is it syntactically accurate and content appropriate?
- Can the individual maintain discussion on a topic or is the person tangential?
- Does the organization of the person's output change when engaged in spontaneous speech versus when responding to a certain set of questions or an agenda structured by another individual (e.g., parent, teacher, peer)? This latter observation of spontaneous versus confrontational speech is important as it can provide clues as to the organizational aspects of verbal output, with the latter being a more challenging task for many individuals following a brain injury.

Relatedly, it becomes important for the evaluator to listen carefully to the individual's speech following a brain injury.
- Is the speech output efficient and fluent or is it dysarthric in nature?
- Is it too fast or too slow in terms of cadence?
- What about the tone of the voice? Is it full of inflections or is it monotonic in nature?
- If the individual is expressing inflections, are they content and affect appropriate or is there a mismatch?

These aspects of vocal prosody are critical to understanding how the speech systems may have been disrupted following a brain injury.

Receptive Language

While expressive language functions are responsible for getting information out in a communicative situation, receptive language functions are responsible for understanding verbal information. Basic receptive language functions include hearing the sounds of a language, the phonemes, and constructing these sounds into words. These functions can be significantly disrupted if the auditory pathways are affected or impaired in any way.

Understanding words or vocabulary is essential to one's receptive language as they lay the foundation for communication. If you don't understand the vocabulary that someone is using, you probably will not fully understand the message that is being conveyed. At its highest level, not only can an individual understand multiple phrases and sentences, but the person can comprehend conflictual and comparative statements that compare and contrast information. As the astute reader will note, higher-order receptive language also requires strong attention/executive capabilities, intact memory functions, and the ability to organize a verbal or nonverbal response.

From an assessment perspective, this is important to recognize because what may present as a receptive language problem actually may be related more to a slippage in attention, a memory problem, or another type of cognitive impairment. Additionally, in many cases, it is not uncommon for an individual to have both receptive and expressive language deficits following a brain injury.

Pragmatic Language

Pragmatic language refers, in large part, to extracting the meaning from different types of language. In most instances, this aligns with the expression and understanding of the social aspects of language. Understanding what someone is saying, despite what words they may be using, is a critical aspect of social functioning. In that regard, pragmatic language abilities are critical to social communication. For example, if language forms such as humor, sarcasm, or other types of idiopathic language were interpreted literally, it is highly likely that an individual would miss the intent of the communication. Similarly, with expressive pragmatics, functions such as correct use of words, appropriate expressive affect and prosody, and turn-taking all impart an understanding of a specific situation. When these elements of communication are "off," it typically is immediately obvious to others involved in the interaction. Sometimes these situations can lead to a misperception of a lack of sensitivity when, in fact, it could be directly related to a pragmatic language impairment.

Additionally, it is important to note that a slow rate of processing for expressive or receptive language pragmatics also can be significantly problematic as the individual will always be a step behind in communication. These types of difficulties are not uncommon following a brain injury, particularly when injuries involve the frontal lobes and/or right hemisphere.

Findings in Children and Adolescents with Traumatic Brain Injury

The incidence of speech and language deficits following a brain injury increases proportionately with the degree of severity (Sullivan & Riccio, 2010). Persistent language disabilities manifest in children injured at younger ages (i.e., less than 5 years of age), and a brain injury can affect the developmental trajectories of language abilities (Ylvisaker & Feeney, 2007). Severe and pervasive deficits, such as mutism and frank aphasias, can be seen in many children following a brain injury, particularly preschool children who have sustained a severe brain injury (Morse et al., 1999; Ylvisaker & Feeney, 2007). More contemporary estimates of aphasic-type disorders secondary to a brain injury have ranged from about one-third of pediatric patients who have been mildly injured to nearly two-thirds of children who have sustained a severe injury (Sullivan & Riccio, 2010), and these disabilities can create significant functional impairments in learning and social arenas. Major impairments also have been reported in expressive language abilities (Hanten et al., 2009), receptive language (Ewing-Cobbs & Barnes, 2002), and pragmatic communication skills, particularly with respect to nonverbal reasoning (Turkstra, McDonald, & Kaufmann, 1996).

In addition to these pervasive types of speech and language impairments, specific language deficits also have been reported. A variety of studies have shown specific impairments in:

- object naming (Barca et al., 2009; Jordan, Ozanne, & Murdoch, 1990);
- verbal fluency (Slater & Bassett, 1988; Winogron et al., 1984);
- word and sentence repetition (Levin & Eisenberg, 1979a, 1979b);
- speech output (Filley et al., 1987);
- syntactic organization (Turkstra & Holland, 1998), and
- linguistic structure (Ewing-Cobbs, Brookshire, Scott, & Fletcher, 1998).

> ...the type of speech and language involvement that will be manifested following a brain injury likely will be related to the language abilities that were in developmental ascendancy at the time of the injury.

The language-based functions of reading and written language also can be significantly impaired following a TBI (Ewing-Cobbs & Barnes, 2002; Ewing-Cobbs, Levin, Eisenberg, & Fletcher, 1987). From a developmental perspective, Ewing-Cobbs, Fletcher, Levin, and Landry (1985) speculated that the type of speech and language involvement that will be manifested following a brain injury likely will be related to the language abilities that were in developmental ascendancy at the time of the injury. In other words, younger children who are still developing their language capabilities are more vulnerable to having their basic language disrupted than an older individual sustaining a similar injury who likely has more advanced language functions. Of course, this speculation is likely to be mediated by the type and severity of the brain injury.

Table 7.1 Representative Subcomponents and Single-Test Language Measures.

Language Subcomponent	Representative Measures
Speech	Goldman-Fristoe-Woodcock Auditory Discrimination Test
	Goldman Speech Discrimination Test
Expressive Language	Controlled Oral Word Association Test (Phonemic and Semantic Categories)
	Boston Naming Test
	Expressive One-Word Picture Vocabulary Test
	Expressive Vocabulary Test
	Comprehensive Assessment of Spoken Language
	Verbal-Motor Production Assessment
	Kaufman Speech Praxis Test
	Test of Word Finding-2
Receptive Language	Peabody Picture Vocabulary Test-4
	Receptive One-Word Picture Vocabulary Test
	Token Test for Children-Revised
	Comprehensive Test of Phonological Processing
	Language Processing Test-3
	Test of Auditory Comprehension of Language-3
Pragmatic Language	Test of Pragmatic Skills
	Test of Language Competence
	Pragmatic Language Skills Inventory
	Test of Pragmatic Language-2
	Test of Problem Solving Skills-3

Additionally, Dennis (1991) noted that the effects of early brain damage on language development and other neurocognitive functions may be apparent for many years following the injury; consequently, the concept of an injury lying "silent" until later developmental time points demands vigilance on the part of the examiner with respect to ongoing developmental surveillance and tracking of language functions over time. Similar sentiments have been echoed by Catroppa and Anderson (2003) in their longitudinal examination of language functioning two years post-injury.

Ewing-Cobbs et al. (1987) studied the language functions of children about six months post mild versus moderate/severe traumatic brain injuries. As a group, they found that not only did a large percentage of their sample manifest significant language impairments, but that expressive difficulties were more prevalent than receptive language problems. Functions most likely to be impaired included naming, repeating sentences, word fluency, writing to dictation, and copying sentences. Few problems were observed on measures of confrontational naming, sentence construction, and auditory comprehension of single words. When the severity groups were examined, they found that the moderate/severe group showed more impairment, particularly on measures of expressive language. Interestingly, no relationships were uncovered with respect to hemispheric involvement.

Assessment Procedures

The above findings point to the importance of including speech and language functions in the overall assessment. This will be important for investigating the impact of a brain injury on language abilities, but also should facilitate where specific interventions will be targeted. The assessment of language functions has been facilitated by the development of practice guidelines for standardized assessment for persons with TBI (Turkstra et al., 2005), along with the availability of a large number of single tests for specific language functions and test batteries that address all of the core language functions noted above. As can be seen in Table 7.1, there are specific tests that assist in the measurement of both receptive and expressive functions.

Example:

One of the best known measures of receptive vocabulary, the Peabody Picture Vocabulary Test, now in its fourth edition (PPVT-IV), has been available to many different clinicians for decades. Not only does this single test measure of receptive vocabulary provide an overall index of an individual's lexicon, but it also can be used for developmental surveillance and ongoing tracking of recovery of function following a brain injury. Its companion, the Expressive Vocabulary Test, provides similar opportunities for assessing expressive vocabulary.

Table 7.2 Representative Language Batteries

Language Batteries
Clinical Evaluation of Language Fundamentals-4
Test of Language Development-2
Test of Language Competence
Preschool Language Test-2
Comprehensive Expressive-Vocabulary Test-Revised
Boston Aphasia Battery

In addition to these single test measures, the language field has produced a large number of test batteries that can provide estimates of both expressive and receptive language functions, as well as provide an overall index of language abilities. Steeped in the aphasia literature, with many of these tasks being developed in the large domain of brain injury (e.g., strokes), many of these test batteries provide a measure of functions across a wide range of development.

As can be seen in Table 7.2, these batteries also provide information pertaining to core language functions (Preschool Language Scale) as well as language pragmatics. For example, one major language battery is the Clinical Evaluation of Language Fundamentals-4 (CELF-4). This battery crosses a large age range and provides estimates of expressive, receptive, and pragmatic language.

There are a variety of other speech and language tasks that are available and it will be important for the evaluator to work closely with a speech and language pathologist in order to obtain a comprehensive assessment of language abilities following a brain injury. This will be particularly important if the child may require augmentative communication equipment and strategies.

Summary

This chapter has provided an overview of critical language abilities, including language pragmatic skills, and findings with respect to how these functions can be disrupted following a brain injury in childhood or adolescence. Given the critical nature of language to communication capabilities and learning, it will be important for these functions to be examined thoroughly following a brain injury—even a mild injury, in conjunction with evidence-based practice guidelines proposed by the Academy of Neurologic Communication Disorders and Sciences (Turkstra et al., 2005). Disruption of language abilities, even a mild and temporary impairment, can disrupt the learning and social functioning of a child in a significant manner. If these difficulties are not uncovered, then those who interact with this individual are left to other interpretations of the child's functioning (e.g., lazy, poor attention, behavior problems). Many of these unfortunate interpretations may further compound the adaptive functioning of that child.

Chapter 8
Visual Processing Functions

Description

With the visual system maturing at a more rapid rate than the language system, many of our visual processing functions tend to develop earlier than our language abilities. As with the linkages between the auditory neurological system and language abilities, there is a direct relationship between the visual neurological system and visual processing functions. Much of this relationship is mediated by neurological systems in the right hemisphere. If there is a disruption in any of the underlying neural networks, then the higher-order visual processing functions become vulnerable to abnormalities as well.

Our visual processing functions help us recognize objects and actions quickly, discriminate between letters, numbers, and various nonverbal cues—including affective expressions. They help us position our bodies in space and construct puzzles and objects into a whole entity when provided with selected cues. Taken together, our visual processing functions contribute to our adaptive problem solving capabilities, and complement our language abilities by providing the nonverbal counterpart in many instances.

Like all of the constructs in this section of the book, visual processing functions are multidimensional in nature. At the most fundamental level is *visual recognition*. This permits an individual to identify colors and objects. *Visual closure* is a special condition wherein an individual recognizes an object when provided with only a few visual cues. *Visual discrimination* helps an individual identify a distinction between different objects in terms of shapes, size, color, etc. *Visual-spatial abilities* facilitate the understanding of our bodies and other objects in space, and in relationship to each other. These functions contribute to our abilities to discriminate between different letters and numbers during our early literacy development, read maps and graphs, engage successfully in various sports, and conduct different types of math problems (e.g., geometry). Our visual recognition and discrimination abilities also allow us to interpret social cues, affective states, and the paralinguistic aspects of communication.

Many of the visual processing functions are linked to two primary pathways through the right hemisphere: the ventral and dorsal pathways. The *ventral pathway* extends from the anterior to posterior regions of the right hemisphere and carries the different forms of visual-spatial information. It has been labeled as the "Where Pathway," given its intimate relationships with spatially-based information.

The *dorsal pathway* also extends from the anterior to posterior regions of the right hemisphere, but carries visual information related to recognition and discrimination. Given these functional features, this neurological route has been labeled the "What Pathway." With damage to the right hemisphere or its neurological connections, these types of impairments can be seen. Given the shearing and tearing of white matter, even at the microscopic level, these types of problems are quite vulnerable to right side brain injuries of any severity.

Findings in children and adolescents with traumatic brain injury

Some of the classic findings from the pediatric brain injury literature extend from work examining nonverbal intellectual functions in children following a traumatic brain injury. Specifically, Chadwick and colleagues (Chadwick, Rutter, Brown, Shaffer, & Traub, 1981; Chadwick, Rutter, Shaffer, & Shrout, 1981) described the presence of depressed Performance IQs in children who sustained a severe closed head injury when compared to children who sustained a mild closed head injury and a group with orthopedic injuries. The various tasks included within the Performance IQ of the Wechsler Intelligence Scales assess visual recognition, visual sequencing, visual organization, visuoconstruction, and higher-order visual-spatial abilities. They also noted that the severely injured group also tended to show a positive rate of recovery of these functions over a 30 month time period.

Using a sample of 20 children who sustained a severe traumatic brain injury, Lehnung et al. (2001) also reported the presence of impaired spatial memory and spatial orientation when compared to a matched control group of children. Further, these investigators found that spatial orientation was disrupted even in individuals who showed intact spatial learning and spatial memory abilities following an injury. Additionally, children who were injured earlier in life showed more impairment than those injured when they were older. Visuoconstructive deficits also have been reported, particularly in copying and construction abilities (Bawden et al., 1985; Chadwick et al., 1981; Klonoff et al., 1977; Levin & Eisenberg, 1979a, 1979b). In fact, Chadwick et al. (1981) noted the presence of these types of difficulties regardless of which hemisphere was affected.

Findings related to the long-standing nature of visual-spatial impairments are mixed. In a four-year follow-up study, Lehnung et al. (2003) found that spatial learning was much improved, but cognitive mapping capabilities remained impaired in their sample with severe traumatic brain injury. Similarly, Thompson et al. (1994) showed ongoing visual-spatial deficits five years post-injury, with a slow developmental trajectory being noted in these abilities for younger children with more severe injuries.

Assessment procedures

The assessment of visual processing abilities is included in nearly all measures of intellectual functioning in some form or fashion. As will be discussed in Chapter 13 (Psychoeducational Assessment), these measures of visual processing encompass:
- tasks assessing visual recognition and visual closure
- two- and three-dimensional visual-spatial abilities
- visuoconstructive and visual organization functions, and
- nonverbal reasoning.

In addition, there are a number of single test measures of visual processing capabilities. For example, as can be seen in Table 8.1, Benton has developed a number of tasks assessing a variety of visual processing abilities. Specifically, these include measures of visual recognition, visual discrimination, and visual-spatial abilities. The Judgment of Line Orientation Test is particularly noteworthy in that it does not require any fine-motor involvement or memory, nor does it place heightened demands on language functions, thus making it a more pure measure of visual-spatial abilities than other tasks such as many of the block design tasks.

As noted above, many of the visual-perceptual tasks are enveloped within nearly all of the intellectual test batteries; however, there are a few nonverbal batteries that include many of these types of tasks. The Wechsler Nonverbal Scale of Ability is designed for individuals ages 4 years of age through 21 years who are struggling with language-related functions. This scale includes the subtests of:
- Matrices
- Object Assembly
- Coding
- Recognition
- Spatial Span, and
- Picture Arrangement.

Table 8.1 Representative Subcomponents and Single-Test Measures of Visual Processing Functions.

Visual Processing Subcomponent	Representative Measures
Visual Recognition	Benton Face Recognition Test
Visual Discrimination and Visual Closure	Benton Line Discrimination Test
Visual-Spatial Abilities	Benton Judgment of Line Orientation Test Matrix Analogies Test Raven's Progressive Matrices
Visual Organization	Hooper Visual Organization Test
Visuoconstructive Abilities	Beery-Buktenicka Developmental Visual-Motor Integration Test Rey-Osterrieth Complex Figure (Copy Condition) Block Construction tasks

Taken together, these subtests assess an array of visual processing abilities including:
- visual recognition
- visual organization
- visual-spatial
- visual memory
- nonverbal reasoning, and
- visual-motor speed.

There also is a short-form comprised of two subtests useful for individuals with short attention spans following a brain injury. Both versions of this scale provide norm-referenced age-based standard scores for the subtests and an overall score. Unlike some of the nonverbal tests, such as the Leiter International Performance Scale-Revised, there is no need for pantomiming the instructions or modified administration procedures. Other nonverbal batteries that largely assess various visual processing and visual-perceptual functions are in Table 8.2.

Summary

From an evaluation perspective, it is important to note that visual processing abilities should be assessed regardless of the severity or type of brain injury. Not only are these functions at risk because of the potential disruption to the visual system, but they are at risk for impairment because of the cortical involvement associated with these types of functions. Specifically, injuries to the frontal regions and/or the right hemisphere place the individual at significant risk for disruption of the "what" and/or "where" pathways in the right hemisphere, as well as the speed of processing and organizational abilities that can be associated with frontal lobe integrity.

Table 8.2 Representative Visual Processing Batteries

Visual Processing Batteries
Wechsler Nonverbal Scale of Ability (Full Battery and Brief Battery)
Test of Visual-Perceptual Skills-Revised
Test of Nonverbal Intelligence-4
Leiter International Performance Scale-3
Universal Nonverbal Intelligence Test

Assessment of the full range of visual processing abilities is critical to understanding the sequelae of a brain injury, particularly as these abilities also will affect specific learning and adaptive capabilities, as well as to track the individual's recovery of function in these areas. Additionally, understanding the profile of visual processing abilities following a traumatic brain injury may provide clues as to what areas may require immediate rehabilitation and intervention. In addition to pediatric neuropsychologists, many occupational therapists have significant expertise in the assessment of visual processing abilities and specific interventions, and it will be important for the evaluator to have a relationship with this interdisciplinary partner.

Chapter 9
Memory and Learning Functions

Description

We need memory functions for nearly everything we do in life. The construct of memory is absolutely essential not only to our learning, but also to our day-to-day adaptive capabilities. Some people have better memory than others. We all forget something during our days and weeks; however, for an individual who sustained a traumatic brain injury, memory may be particularly problematic. This is complicated by the fact that the neurological systems for memory are located in many different parts of the brain. Suffice it to say that, as with all of the neurocognitive constructs discussed in this section, memory is complex and multidimensional in nature. Consequently, memory is not a single function but, rather, many different functions. At its most basic level, our memory functions are responsible for storing information (e.g., facts, procedures, faces), retrieving information in an efficient fashion, and regulating information during its recall and retrieval (i.e., working memory).

When we think about the different types of memory, there are a variety of ways to examine the components of memory. First, memory can be examined by modality. The most common types of memory that are mentioned in the literature are ***visual memory*** and ***auditory memory***, but we also have memory tied to our other senses as well. We all have ***tactile memory***, ***gustatory memory***, and ***olfactory memory***. Interestingly, given that the olfactory nerve truncates deep in the temporal region near the hippocampi, there are many memories that can be triggered by sense of smell.

Second, there is a time dimension that is critical to memory such that we have short-term and long-term recall. ***Short-term memory*** relates to items that you do not intend to use more than once, or perhaps a few times. Short-term memory is evidenced in our day-to-day lives when we try to remember a phone number long enough to insert it into a smart phone, or to recall a hotel room number on a trip; however, once the phone number is stored in your smart phone or you have long left the hotel, these are items that you probably won't remember.

In contrast, ***long-term memory*** is employed when we need to hold on to information for a long period of time, such as names, faces, rules, or mathematical formulae. Once the information is processed in short-term memory, then it is placed in our long-term storage. A form of long-term memory, ***remote memory***, pertains to information that is retrieved by an individual years or even decades after the information first entered short-term memory. These "file cabinets" of information, if organized, can be retrieved efficiently when needed or cued.

> **At their most basic level, our memory functions are responsible for storing information (e.g., facts, procedures, faces), retrieving information in an efficient fashion, and regulating information during its recall and retrieval (i.e., working memory).**

Finally, it may appear that these informational units are no longer present following a brain injury, but in many instances this difficulty with *retrieval* may be related more to the disorganization created by the brain injury than to an elimination of this information. Although all of these types of retrieval tend to occur without most people even being aware of them, developing strategies to access this information will be important therapeutic considerations following a traumatic brain injury.

With respect to the recall of information, and following its encoding and routing through short-term memory, there are several ways that information is retrieved. At the most basic level is *recognition memory*, which is the lowest form of memory. Here, information is retrieved by "recognizing" something that you have seen or heard before. This is one of the reasons why many individuals prefer multiple choice and matching types of tests in school as they are largely dependent on recognition memory. Similarly, once something is so ingrained in memory and, perhaps practiced repeatedly, it becomes automatic (e.g., writing your name). This *automatic memory* occurs very rapidly, typically without thinking. For motor skills, Luria (1966) referred to this type of memory as a kinetic melody.

There also are a number of other types of recall that include *episodic and nonepisodic memory*, where the emphasis is placed on events that happened to you (episodes) versus other types of events, respectively. The idea here is that information that is contextualized or relevant to you will have a better chance of being recalled than information that is not contextualized. Declarative and procedural types of memory relate to different types of information that need to be *recalled*. *Declarative memory* relates to the recall of facts, while *procedural recall* pertains to the recall of procedures, or ways to do things.

Understanding the different types of memory and retrieval is important to the assessment process as making comparisons between the different kinds of memory can provide clues as to what memory systems are disrupted.

Example:
If the attention mechanisms are disrupted, perhaps information is not even being processed in short-term memory. In this instance, a memory problem may be secondary to an attention deficit.
- ☐ Once information is encoded, can it be retrieved?
- ☐ If so, is there a difference between short-term recall versus long-term recall?
- ☐ If the difficulty is with retrieval, does the individual respond to different types of strategies, such as multiple repetitions, semantic cues, or associative learning, or do strategies involving recognition memory need to be initiated?
- ☐ What is the profile of recall across the different modalities?

These types of comparisons will increase the understanding of the impact of a traumatic brain injury on the different memory functions and, hopefully, provide avenues to treatment for the memory challenges that are present as the individual moves through the recovery process. Understanding the neurological basis for many of our memory functions also permits using these profiles to assist in localizing the injury and tracking the recovery of function.

Findings in Children and Adolescents with Brain Injury

Memory problems following a brain injury of any severity are reported rather frequently across the age span, with some evidence suggesting that males may be more prone to memory disruption than females (Donders & Hoffman, 2002; Moore, Ashman, Cantor, Krinick, & Spielman, 2009), and that these deficits can linger for long periods of time post-injury (e.g. Levin et al., 1988). The literature on adults is reasonably clear in showing lateralization of memory dysfunction wherein left temporal dysfunction is more related to verbal memory impairment and right temporal lobe involvement is more related to visual memory deficits.

This strong lateralization pattern is less clear for children, with contemporary evidence suggesting diffuse axonal injury and cortical thinning, particularly in the frontal and anterior temporal regions, being most associated with recall difficulties for both mildly injured (Geary, Kraus, Pliskin, & Little, 2010; Wu et al., 2010) and moderately to severely injured children (Kramer, Chiu, Shear, & Wade, 2009; McCauley et al., 2010; Salorio et al., 2005). In this regard, a variety of memory problems can be seen following a brain injury in children or adolescents (Allen et al., 2010). Similar to other functional domains, the presence of memory deficits secondary to milder brain injuries is less clear, especially over the long term, while their presence is much clearer in children sustaining moderate or severe brain injuries.

A number of investigators have demonstrated overall memory difficulties in samples of children and adolescents with moderate to severe brain injuries. Allen et al. (2010) demonstrated global memory deficits on the Test of Memory and Learning (TOMAL) when compared to nonbrain injury controls. On average, individuals with TBI were 1.3 standard deviations below the controls on all of the TOMAL measures. Yeates, Blumenstein, Patterson, and Delis (1995) demonstrated similar findings within the verbal memory domain, with the pattern of deficits being related to the severity of the injury. Specifically, Yeates et al. (1995) noted that children who sustained a mild to moderate injury were equal to controls on the learning trials, but struggled with delayed retrieval of information. Children with severe injuries showed pervasive verbal memory and learning difficulties when compared to controls, and they exhibited significantly more intrusion errors than the group with mild to moderate TBI.

> **Understanding the different types of memory and retrieval is important to the assessment process as making comparisons between the different kinds of memory can provide clues as to what memory systems are disrupted.**

In contrast, Nolin (2006) showed that children with a mild brain injury were less likely to use the strategy of semantic clustering than controls, expressed an increased number of intrusion errors, and struggled with recognition memory more than their uninjured counterparts. How these different types of memory change as an individual moves through the recovery process remains unexplored, but not surprisingly it does appear that severity of injury does have an affect on the recovery process (Anderson & Catroppa, 2007).

In addition to global memory impairments following various injury severity levels, there have been a number of reports pointing to specific types of memory impairments following a TBI. In this regard specific impairments have been reported for:

- Once information is encoded, can it be retrieved?
- selective verbal learning, where children with severe TBI performed more poorly than a comparison group of typically developing children (Hanten, Zhang, & Levin, 2002);
- explicit memory, where children with moderate to severe TBI performed more poorly than controls, but at a level equal to controls on procedural memory (Ward, Shum, Wallace, & Boon, 2002); and
- contextualized memory, where children with severe TBI performed more poorly than controls across immediate, delayed, and recognition trials (Josman, Berney, & Jarus, 2000).

Declarative memory (i.e., recall of facts and events) impairments also have been routinely reported in children and adolescents who have sustained a traumatic brain injury, with these types of impairment remaining present in over 25% of children following a severe traumatic brain injury (Levin & Hanten, 2002). This type of memory is comprised of two components:

- retrospective memory (i.e., recall of previously learned information) and
- prospective memory (i.e., the ability to recall future actions and intentions).

While much of the work to date has focused on the retrospective form of declarative memory, the other form, prospective memory, has begun to receive increased attention in recent years (Shum, Levin, & Chan, 2011). These types of memory impairments have been reported in mild TBI in children (Ward, Shum, Dick, McKinlay, & Baker-Tweney, 2004; Tay, Ang, Lau, Meyyappan, & Collinson, 2010), suggesting that this type of memory problem should be assessed following even a mild brain injury, as well as in those sustaining a more severe brain injury (McCauley et al., 2010; McCauley & Levin, 2011). Further, emergent evidence also indicates that the degree of memory deficit might be related to increased cognitive load or memory complexity (Ward, Shum, McKinlay, Baker, & Wallace, 2007).

Assessment procedures

Given the array of memory deficits that have been reported in children and adolescents following a brain injury, a thorough assessment of memory functions appears to be in order (Lajiness-O'Neill, Erdodi, & Bigler, 2010). This is not only because of the vulnerability to injury of key structures related to memory secondary to their location in the skull (e.g., left and right hippocampi), but because of how the memory system interacts with other key cognitive abilities such as attention, language, and executive functions. These inter-relationships also implicate the need for other types of assessment to complement an assessment of memory. For example, given the high degree of association between memory and attention, the careful examiner should always consider obtaining an assessment of attention along with their measures of memory functions.

Table 9.1 Representative Subcomponents and Single-Test Measures of Memory Functions.

Memory Modality	Representative Measures
Verbal Memory and Learning	Children's Auditory-Verbal Learning Test
	California Verbal Learning Test-Children's Version
	Rey-Auditory Verbal Learning Test
	Benton Sentence Memory Test
	Buschke Verbal Selective Reminding Test
Visual Memory and Learning	Rey-Osterrieth Complex Figure (Delay Condition
	Nonverbal Selective Reminding Test
	Benton Visual Retention Test

In this regard, there are a variety of single tests for memory (Table 9.1), although these tests tend to provide a wide array of scores that yield information on many different aspects of memory. One frequently administered memory test is the California Verbal Learning Test (CVLT). The CVLT comes in both child and adult versions, and is administered by reciting a word list that the individual is required to remember. The individual can remember the information in any order. This process is repeated five straight times, with the idea being that recall should improve with repetition. Once the five trials are completed, then a second word list, the distracter list, is presented one time and the individual is required to recall words from that list. Following this trial, the individual is then asked to reproduce as many words as possible from the first list, and then asked to provide words from the first list that fall into designated categories (e.g., fruits, clothing).

After approximately a 20 minute delay, these latter two tasks are re-administered and the person is given a recognition trial. Age-based standardized scores are provided for a variety of indices. The CVLT provides indices for short-term memory, delayed recall, learning rate, cued recall, verbal recognition, and a number of other important memory-related scores. These indices have proven useful in diagnosing a memory impairment following a brain injury as well as in tracking the recovery of memory functions (e.g., Donders, 1993; Warschausky, Kay, Chi, & Donders, 2005). Scores from the CVLT are not only sensitive to TBI severity, they also have been shown to be predictive of educational outcomes in this pediatric population.

The profile of verbal memory abilities, in tandem with the observation of what strategies are being used (e.g., serial recall) and what specific strategies may improve recall (e.g., repetition, semantic cues) should facilitate the development of intervention programs. These types of findings and observations will be critical to understanding the full impact of a brain injury on a child's memory and learning. Several examples of single memory tests, organized by verbal and visual modality, can be seen in Table 9.1

In addition to the availability of single test approaches to memory assessment, over the past 20 years the number of memory batteries also has expanded, thus making a comprehensive memory assessment more readily available. Additionally, some memory batteries provide standardized measures of attention as part of the memory assessment, thus obviating the need for additional measures of attention in a larger assessment battery. For example, the Wide Range Assessment of Memory and Learning (WRAML-2), the Children's Memory Scale (CMS), and the Test of Memory and Learning-2 (TOMAL-2) provide indices for short-term and delayed recall of visual and verbal materials along with measures of attention. Similar to many of the single test measures of memory, nearly all of the memory batteries provide avenues for understanding what strategies may be most useful to facilitate an individual's recall. For example, the TOMAL-2 provides not only strategies examining multiple repetition, but also associative learning. Findings from these batteries have been linked to severity of injury and nature of the injury (e.g., diffuse lesions, right cerebral focal lesions) (Lowther & Mayfield, 2004; Woodward & Donders, 1998). Examples of these memory batteries can be seen in Table 9.2.

Table 9.2 Representative Memory Batteries.

Memory Batteries
Wechsler Memory Scale-4
Wide Range Assessment of Memory and Learning-2
Children's Memory Scale
Test of Memory and Learning-2
Visual-Aural Digit Span Test

> ... given the high degree of association between memory and attention, the careful examiner should always consider obtaining an assessment of attention along with their measures of memory functions.

Summary

In general, the literature suggests the presence of memory impairments as a common finding in children and adolescents following a traumatic brain injury. Consequently, the assessment of memory functions will be a critical component of any type of evaluation following a moderate to severe injury, although the presence of memory dysfunction in milder types of injuries should not be overlooked. Further, the assessment of memory should be complemented by measures of other cognitive functions, most notably attention and executive functions, so as to determine the involvement of these functions in the memory impairment. Additionally, memory assessment should be part of any ongoing surveillance of cognitive status as memory impairments can be long-lasting deficits, particularly for children and adolescents with more severe injuries and/or a younger age of injury.

Chapter 10
Executive Functions

Description

Of all of the neurocognitive constructs, this one is probably the most complex. The complexity comes not only in its overall regulatory functions, but also in how executive functions interact with nearly every other neurocognitive function. In general, executive processes have been deemed critical to the integrity of many learning and social-behavioral functions (Jefferson, Paul, Ozonoff, & Cohen, 2006; Mazzocco & Kover, 2007; Riggs, Jahromi, Razza, Dilworth-Bart, & Mueller, 2006; Rutherford, Young, Hepburn, & Rogers, 2006). There are a number of definitions of executive functions, some extending back nearly 50 years (Luria, 1966), but the definition by Welsh and Pennington (1988) captures nearly all of the features of this multidimensional domain.

Executive function is primarily the set maintenance required to achieve a future goal. This set would include the requisite skills of planning, organization, inhibition of maladaptive responses, self-monitoring, and flexibility of strategies contingent on feedback (p. 200).

As can be surmised from the above definition, executive functions are generally viewed within a multidimensional framework of cognitive abilities that provide critical support for goal-directed, future-oriented behaviors (Zelazo & Muller, 2010; Zelazo, Muller, Frye, & Marcovitch, 2003). These behaviors typically include (Anderson, 2002; Barkley, 2001; Miyake et al., 2000; Pennington, 1997; Zelazo et al., 2003):

- ☐ attention regulation (see Chapter 6)
- ☐ inhibitory control
- ☐ working memory
- ☐ set shifting/cognitive flexibility
- ☐ planning, and
- ☐ cognitive efficiency

The multiple dimensions of executive functions have been embedded within conceptual and empirical models (Krasnegor & Lyon, 1996; Zelazo & Muller, 2010) that comprise two (Carlson, Moses, & Claxton, 2004); three (Hughes, 1998; Pennington, 1997; Welsh, Pennington, & Groisser, 1991), four (Denckla, 1996; Espy, Kaufmann, McDiarmid, & Glisky, 1999; Stuss, 2007), and six factors (Daigneault, Braun, & Whitaker, 1992).

There are notable differences between these models, but there also are a number of specific executive functions that appear across the models. For example, planning and problem solving, inhibitory control, set shifting, and set maintenance usually are included in some fashion in many of these models. Additionally, speeded responding and working memory have been discussed as subcomponents of executive function. In particular, working memory has been included under the different types of memory but, given its regulatory functions, it typically is discussed under executive functions (Goldman-Rakic & Friedman, 1991).

Most of these functions are linked to the dorsolateral prefrontal cortex and associated brain regions, but it is important to remember that the

> **Consequently, an injury during any of these periods of developmental ascendency will have an effect on specific functions along with the developmental trajectories of these functions.**

emotional control functions associated with the ventromedial prefrontal cortex also should be included in a larger executive function model. This will be especially important for increasing our understanding of the neurobehavioral difficulties presented by many children and adolescents following a brain injury (see Chapter 11).

Additionally, all of the various executive functions will have differential effects on learning and behavior over time, with a sequential unfolding of various executive functions over the course of development (Grattan & Eslinger, 1991). Specifically, while executive functions appear to develop from infancy into early adulthood, it appears that the period of most rapid development occurs between the ages of 6 and 8 years of age followed by more modest gains between the ages of 9 and 12. Continued, but differential development continues through adolescence into early adulthood depending on the specific task or behavior of interest (Anderson, Anderson, Northam, Jacobs, & Catroppa, 2001; Korkman, Kemp, & Kirk, 2001; MacNeill, Soper, & Reynolds, 2010; Romine & Reynolds, 2005; Welsh et al., 1991). Consequently, an injury during any of these periods of developmental ascendency will have an effect on specific functions along with the developmental trajectories of these functions.

Finally, from a neurological perspective, executive functions have been linked to specific underlying brain regions, particularly the dorsolateral prefrontal cortex (Barcelo & Knight, 2002; Knight, 2002; Levine, Stuss, Milberg, Alexander, Schwartz, & MacDonald, 1998; Miller & Tomarken, 2001; Petrides, 2000) and the ventromedial regions of the orbitofrontal cortex (Bechara, Damasio, & Damasio, 2000; Berns, McClure, Pagnoni, & Montague, 2001; Knutson, Fong, Adams, Varner, & Hommer, 2001; Mesulam, 2002; Montague, 2002; Rolls, 2004). The so called "cool functions of the dorsolateral prefrontal cortex represent the executive functions of motor planning and regulation, integration of sensory and mnemonic information, working memory, and attention regulation (Hongwanishkul, Happaney, Lee, & Zelazo, 2005). The ventromedial regions of the orbitofrontal cortex are involved in planning and decision-making, but they also mediate affective regulatory functions, or the so called "hot" functions (Hongwanishkul et al., 2005).

Disruption to subcomponents of any of these regions of the prefrontal cortex could trigger specific executive dysfunctions in cognitive and/or behavioral-emotional functioning. Given the developmental trajectories of many of these functions, it also is possible for an earlier injury to "lie silent" until they are developmentally required, and a specific executive dysfunction could emerge at a later developmental epoch (e.g., during middle school). This can create the apparent emergence of a "new" learning or behavior problem, and requires that evaluators routinely inquire about brain injuries in their developmental history for any given case.

Findings in children and adolescents with brain injuries

Along with attention impairments, one of the most common findings in pediatric traumatic brain injury is the presence of various types of executive dysfunction (Chevignard, Catroppa, Galvin, & Anderson, 2010; Levin & Hanten, 2005). These types of problems have been reported across the age span as well as injury severity levels, with younger and/or more severely injured children showing greater impairments in executive functions.

Recently, Whitney-Sesma, Slomine, Ding, and McCarthy (2008) found that their group of children with mild to severe pediatric brain injury showed more executive dysfunction on the Behavior Rating Inventory of Executive Functions (BRIEF) Global Executive Composite at three months post injury than their orthopedic comparison group. These differences persisted to include all three summary scales of the BRIEF at the one year follow-up. In particular, the Working Memory Scale differentiated between all of the groups at both time points. These investigators noted that 18% to 38% of the children with traumatic brain injury were described by their parents as manifesting significant executive dysfunction in the first year post injury, with children with more severe injuries receiving ratings reflecting more executive function impairment. A similar pattern of abilities was reported by parents of children with severe TBI five years post-injury, with these executive function ratings being associated with children's psychiatric status, family burden, and general family functioning. Using the BRIEF, Maillard-Wermelinger et al. (2009) showed a similar trend for children with a mild TBI, although results were not as striking. Additionally, Wilson, Donders, and Nhuyen (2011) found that adolescents with severe TBI tended to report fewer problems in executive functioning, particularly in their metacognitive abilities, than parents; consequently, evaluators should be aware of such differences in rating scales when working with children and their families.

Other empirical studies have documented the presence of impairments in planning and problem solving (Levin, Song, Ewing-Cobbs, & Roberson, 2001; Pentland, Todd, & Anderson, 1998); abstract thinking and analogical reasoning (Krawezyk et al., 2010); set-shifting and cognitive flexibility (Yeates et al., 2005; Ward et al., 2007); inhibitory control (Leblanc et al., 2005; Levin, Hanten, Zhang, Swank, & Hunter, 2004); metacognitive capabilities (Hanten et al., 2004; Hanten, Bartha, & Levin, 2000); processing speed (Prigatano, Gray, & Gale, 2008); and working memory (Chapman et al., 2006; Conklin, Salorio, & Slomine, 2008; Ewing-Cobbs, Prasad, Landry, Kramer, & DeLeon, 2004; Levin et al., 2004; Mandalis, Kinsella, Ong, & Anderson, 2007; Moran, Nippold, & Gillon, 2006; Newsome et al., 2008). Additionally, as noted earlier (Chapter 7), higher-order language impairments also have been reported such that pragmatic skills in both expressive and receptive language are disrupted (Moran et al., 2006).

In general, following a traumatic brain injury, nearly all of these executive functioning components will evidence a degree of impairment that is dictated, in part, by the severity of the brain injury. These deficits also have been reported to be persistent in some fashion seven to ten years post injury (Muscara, Catroppa, & Anderson, 2008).

Finally, in conjunction with what is known about the regulatory role of the ventromedial prefrontal cortex in social and affective functions, a number of studies have begun to assess the role of self-regulation and social cognition in children following a traumatic brain injury.

Ganesalingam, Sanson, Anderson, & Yeates (2007) utilized a sample of children with moderate to severe brain injuries who were two to five years post injury and examined their performance on self-regulation tasks and social-behavioral functioning. They reported that the children with brain injuries showed significantly more difficulties in these functions than a match control group. These investigators also demonstrated that self-regulatory abilities served as mediators of the effects of traumatic brain injury and the emergence of social-behavioral difficulties in this population.
In addition to difficulties in self-regulatory functions, children sustaining a TBI have evidenced problems identifying emotions (Turkstra et al., 2001), labeling emotions (Tlustos et al., 2011), extracting meaning from nonliteral social communication (Dennis, Purvis, Barnes, Wilkinson, & Winner, 2001), and evaluating problem solving outcomes (Janusz, Kirkwood, Yeates, & Taylor, 2002). In fact, many of these deficits have been reported up to four years post injury (Dennis et al., 2001; Janusz et al., 2002).

Assessment Procedures

Given the strong association of these executive functions with the frontal regions of the brain and the vulnerability of these regions to damage following a traumatic brain injury, these neurocognitive functions, in whole or in part, are at risk for impairment following a brain injury. Consequently, the inclusion of these functions in any assessment of neurocognitive abilities should be considered. In this regard, the assessment of executive functioning has made enormous strides over the past two decades. In the past, there were few instruments available to clinicians—even neuropsychologists—for the assessment of executive functions. This was accentuated by the lack of training in assessment of these various abilities. Over the past 20 years or so, however, the assessment of executive functions has seen the development of a number of tools, many of which are normatively based, standardized, and span a wide age range—including preschool children. In fact, more recently, assessment tools even have been developed to assess executive functioning using qualitative approaches in an effort to have these tasks be more ecologically valid.

For example, Chevignard, Catroppa, Galvin, and Anderson (2010) examined the quality of executive functions in children with mild and moderate-severe TBI using The Children's Cooking Task. This was an adaptation of an adult task that was designed to determine the child's ability to follow a checklist without being distracted, evaluate the outcomes with respect to the initial goals for cooking, and make adjustments for any errors, Here, the task was comprised of actually making a chocolate cake and a fruit cocktail, and the task is performed in a kitchen. Variables of interest from this task include the number of errors and an overall qualitative analysis of the task. As expected, Chevignard et al. (2010) found that all children with traumatic brain injury made more errors in the cooking process as compared to aged matched controls. Other qualitative tasks that involve real-life simulations include video-taped vignettes of social situations (Turkstra et al., 2001), the Party Planning Task (Pentland, Todd, & Anderson, 1998), the Child-Kitchen Task (Rocke, Hays, Edwards, & Berg, 2008), and the School Assessment of Motor and Process Skills (Atchison, Fisher, & Bryze, 1998). From a school-based perspective, this latter task provides an assessment of the skills that children need to function in the classroom setting, and holds promise for inclusion in executive function appraisals.

There are a number of more standardized measures that provide estimates of selected executive functions, and more recently executive function batteries and ratings scales have been developed. When one considers the various subcomponents of executive functions, there are:

☐ measures of inhibitory control (e.g., errors of commission on the continuous performance tests, Matching Familiar Figures Test, Go No-Go tasks, Stop Signal Test);
☐ speeded responding (e.g., rapid naming tasks, motor sequencing tasks, verbal fluency tasks such as Controlled Oral Word Association Test, nonverbal fluency tasks such as the Ruff Nonverbal Fluency Test);
☐ planning and problem solving (e.g., Wisconsin Card Sorting Test Categories Correct, Tower of Hanoi, Tower of London, Porteus Mazes);
☐ set maintenance and perseveration (e.g., Wisconsin Card Sorting Test Perseveration Score);
☐ set-shifting (e.g., Stroop Color and Word Test, Wisconsin Card Sorting Test);
☐ working memory (e.g., Digit Span, Spatial Span); and
☐ attention regulation (e.g., CPT Variability Scores).

Additionally, as noted above, there are now relatively new measures available to assess selected executive functions in the preschool population, with tasks going down to two years of age. Several of these tasks include the Shape School (Espy et al., 2004), which assesses inhibitory control; the IS Task (Jacques & Zelazo, 2001), which measures set-shifting; working memory span (Kane & Engle, 2003); and the Tower Task (Kochanska et al., 1996), which assesses planning/and problem solving. Several of the continuous performance tests (e.g., Kiddie Conners CPT) also are available for use for children ages 3 to 5. A review of the tasks, along with emergent psychometric properties can be found in Carlson (2005) and Willoughby, Blair, Wirth, and Greenberg (2010). A representative listing of single test measures for the various executive functions can be seen in Table 10.1.

Table 10.1 Representative Subcomponents and Single-Test Executive Function Measures.

Executive Function Subcomponent	Representative Measures
Planning and Problem Solving	Wisconsin Card Sorting Test (Categories Correct) Tower of Hanoi Tower of London Porteus Mazes Test of Problem Solving Skills
Inhibitory Control	Matching Familiar Figures Test GoNoGo Tasks CPT Errors of Commission Shape School
Set-Shifting	Stroop Color and Word Test IS Task Trail-Making Test Part B
Set Maintenance	Wisconsin Card Sorting Test (Perseveration Score)
Speeded Responding	Rapid Naming Tasks Controlled Oral Word Association Test Ruff Figural Fluency Test Motor Sequencing Tasks Trail-Making Test (Parts A & B) Simple Reaction Time Tasks
Working Memory	Working Memory Battery Subtests Digit Span Spatial Span
Attention Regulation	Conners Continuous Performance Test-II Kiddie Conners Continuous Performance Test Test of Variables of Attention Gordon Diagnostic System
Affective Regulation	Diagnostic Assessment of Nonverbal Abilities CANTAB Affective Go No-Go Subtest

Finally, all of the above tasks will provide estimates of functions associated with the dorsolateral prefrontal cortex. Although the assessment of emotional and behavioral regulation has been assessed in the laboratory for a number of years, there still are few well normed and standardized tests that provide an assessment of this critical component of executive function that have crossed over into the clinical realm. Of course, these types of dysregulation are described by both parents and children in the clinical interview, and there are a number of rating scales that can provide an indication of such problems (see Chapter 11). Nonetheless, several assessment tasks have begun to appear that will assist in this aspect of the assessment.

One of these tasks is the Affective Go No-Go task from the computerized Cambridge Neuropsychological Automated Battery. On this task, the individual is asked to inhibit responses to selected targets. Another recent addition to this list has been the Diagnostic Assessment of Nonverbal Abilities (DANVA). The DANVA is a computerized battery that provides estimates of emotional regulation and control, thus providing some assessment of the ventromedial prefrontal cortex integrity. On the DANVA, the individual is asked to perform several tasks that address affective recognition and discordance via visual and auditory pathways. Scores provide an indication of both receptive and expressive affective regulation.

In addition to the single test measures of specific executive functions, there have been several batteries and rating scales put forward that provide standardized, normative approaches for children and adolescents. One of these batteries, the Delis-Kaplan Executive Function System (D-KEFS, Delis et al, 2001), provides an array of executive function tasks that have been normed and standardized on the same population. Having an entry level of age 8 and extending well into adulthood, the D-KEFS contains eight different subtests that can be administered in whole or in part. These subtests assess set-shifting while controlling for fine-motor speed, verbal and nonverbal fluency, inhibitory control, planning and problem solving, abstract thinking, and cognitive flexibility. A similar executive function battery, the Behavioural Assessment of the Dysexecutive Syndrome for Children (BADS-C; Emslie, Wilson, Burden, Nimmo-Smith, & Wilson, 2003), is a downward extension of an adult battery, and can be used for children ages 8 to 16 years.

A final approach to the assessment of executive functions is the rating scale approach. To date, there are several ratings scales available to assess executive functioning in children and adolescents:
- the Dysexecutive Questionnaire for Children (DEX-C), which is part of the larger Behavioural Assessment of the Dysexecutive Syndrome for Children (BADS-C; Emslie et al., 2003);
- Behavior Rating Inventory of Executive Function (BRIEF; Gioia, Isquith, Guy, & Kenworthy, 2000);
- Comprehensive Executive Function Inventory (CEFI; Naglieri & Goldstein, 2013); and
- Delis-Rating of Executive Functions (Delis, 2012).

These measures are not direct assessment batteries per se, but rather comprehensive rating scales that provide estimates of both cognitive and affective regulatory functions in a multi-rater, multi-setting framework. For example, for the BRIEF, there is a preschool version, a school-age version, and an adult self-report version, thus providing a mechanism to follow executive functions through recovery and across the age span from preschool into adulthood. Like all ratings scales, the BRIEF (and the other rating scales) is subject to attribution bias and responder acquiescence, but it can provide useful information on the application of executive functions in the child's ecology. To illustrate, on the School Age BRIEF, in addition to three overall summary indices (Metacognitive Index, Behavioral Regulation Index, Global Executive Composite), there are eight different empirically derived scales measuring various aspects of executive function. These include:
- Inhibit
- Shift
- Emotional Control
- Initiate
- Working memory
- Plan/organize
- Organization of materials and
- Monitor.

Rating scale approaches provide a time effective alternative to direct assessment, and they also may provide a different type of (ecological) information pertaining to executive functioning in children with TBI (Gioia & Isquith, 2004).

Summary

The assessment of executive functions has come a long way over the past two decades, with many measures moving out of the laboratory and into the clinical setting. Even with these advances, though, the assessment of executive functions typically is not conducted as part of a routine psychoeducational or psychological evaluation, or as part of other types of evaluation (e.g., speech and language, occupational therapy, etc.). Given the relatively high prevalence of

> **Consequently, it is essential for the examiner to include executive function measures as part of any assessment of a child following a traumatic brain injury.**

frontal lobe involvement in children and adolescents who have sustained a brain injury—even a mild injury—this oversight could leave a significant hole in the overall neurocognitive profile of an individual following a traumatic brain injury.

Further, given the regulatory aspects of many of the executive functions, it is not uncommon to see expressive and receptive language, sensory-motor functions, or academic achievement skills appearing to be unaffected by a brain injury, yet the child is not able to access the preserved information accurately and/or efficiently secondary to executive dysfunction. Without the assessment of executive functions, those working with the child are left with other plausible, but possibly incorrect assumptions about the nature of the child's capabilities (e.g., lazy, unmotivated, uninterested, behavioral problems, etc.).

Consequently, it is essential for the examiner to include executive function measures as part of any assessment of a child following a traumatic brain injury. As a final note, it is suspected that the administration, scoring, and interpretation of executive function measures are rarely taught across the various professional training programs (e.g., clinical psychology, school psychology, speech and language, occupational therapy, etc.) and, from a training perspective, it is imperative that these types of assessment procedures become a larger part of these training programs. This is important not only from an assessment perspective, but also with respect to how executive dysfunctions can impact therapeutic initiatives with children following a traumatic brain injury.

Chapter 11
Social-Behavioral Functions

Description

Social, emotional, and behavioral functioning represents a wide range of human expression. These functions represent the use of selected skills in specific social situations, facilitate how we feel about different events and experiences, and how we react under a variety of different conditions. Typically functioning individuals will evidence a wide range of emotions and exhibit situationally appropriate social skills and related behaviors. When these functions are disturbed in any way, interactions with family, friends, and the outside environment will be different and, in some instances, impaired. From an assessment perspective, there are a number of ways to approach these social, emotional, and behavioral issues, but from the vantage point of traumatic brain injury, a neuropsychiatric approach that provides diagnoses and specific symptom descriptions may be most meaningful.

Psychiatric Disorders

One way to begin to organize these variants in social, emotional, and behavioral functioning pertains to psychiatric classification. Over the past three decades or more, the classification of childhood and adolescent psychopathology has evolved such that there are now specific criteria for a large array of specific diagnoses. This has been fueled by ongoing developments of the Diagnostic and Statistical Manual of Mental Disorders-V (APA, 2013), the International Classification of Diseases, and recognition of such problems in educational settings under the classification of Emotional and Behavioral Disturbed (or whatever designation your state or territory uses). While the educational classification system tends to be rather unidimensional in its approach, the ICD and DSM systems provide criteria for clinicians to diagnose depression and other affective disorders, thought disorders such as schizophrenia, disruptive behavior disorders such as conduct disorder and ADHD, anxiety disorders, substance abuse, and a number of other psychiatric difficulties (e.g., eating disorders, tic disorders, etc.). Despite these advances, there are a number of issues and challenges with asserting an accurate diagnosis as well as with the associated reliability and validity of specific diagnoses. In that regard, dimensional classification approaches have evolved over the past six decades or so.

> Over the past three decades or more, the classification of childhood and adolescent psychopathology has evolved such that there are now specific criteria for a large array of specific diagnoses.

Dimensional Classifications

In contrast to the categorical approach of the DSM or ICD systems, this approach to psychiatric classification utilizes empirically derived dimensions of childhood and adolescent psychopathology (i.e., homogeneous groups of behaviors that are statistically inter-correlated). A diagnostic profile can then be determined by plotting the child's score for each dimension in relation to normative data (e.g., Achenbach & Edelbrock, 1983). One major characteristic of dimensional classification systems is their relatively strong reliability, which tends to be a by-product of the statistical derivation of the dimensions and contributes to stability of ratings across different raters and clinical populations of children.

To illustrate, the dimensional classification system by Achenbach (2010) provides for two major problem dimensions: internalizing problem behaviors and externalizing problem behaviors. Internalizing problem behaviors largely relate to behaviors that are affective in their manifestation. Given their inward expression, these behaviors tend to relate to disorders such as depression and anxiety, along with social withdrawal and avoidance. In contrast, externalizing problem behaviors are largely related to behaviors that are externally expressed. These behaviors tend to be more associated with disorders such as ADHD, conduct disorder, and socially inappropriate or antisocial types of behavior. Taken together, this wide constellation of behaviors can capture much of the social, emotional, and behavioral residuals following a traumatic brain injury, and can provide age-adjusted normative data from which to describe the severity of these behaviors at different points in the recovery process.

Neuroaffective Models

As noted in the discussion of executive functions in Chapter 10, the ventromedial prefrontal cortex and associated neurological regions play a significant role in the regulation of affective reception and expression. The neurological systems within this region of the brain contribute to how reward is perceived and managed, and to how these systems interact with other key cortical and subcortical connections.

There has been increasing scientific interest in how affective processing occurs in the brain, both from receptive and expressive perspectives. Specific neurological models have emerged over the past 30 years. Such models have evolved from the study of the lateralization of emotion and the localization of cerebral regulatory mechanisms for affect in both humans (e.g., Flor-Henry, 1979) and animals (e.g., Denenberg, 1983), to the more contemporary efforts to examine specific brain structures and functions with advanced neuroimaging techniques (e.g., Ewings-Cobbs et al., 2008; Gale & Prigatano, 2010).

Earlier efforts to understand affective processing identified the right hemisphere as being critical to the expression and perception of human emotions, with the anterior regions being largely responsible for mediating the expression of affect and the posterior region being responsible for the reception of emotions (Bryden, 1982; Davidson, 1993). For example, Tucker's (1992) model of emotional functioning was perhaps one of the most robust at that time, noting that the right hemisphere provided a control mechanism for both the perceptual and arousal systems in the brain such that disruption to this system would contribute to variability in an individual's emotional tone and responsiveness.

More contemporary models of emotional functioning have attempted to take into account the influence of affective processing and its underlying neural systems in trying to understand how such information is expressed and processed, and what happens when something goes wrong (e.g., a brain injury). For example, one model that considers the relationship between cognitive functions and affect is the Cognitive-Affective Processing System (CAPS; Shoda & Smith, 2004). By examining the interaction between cognition and affect, issues pertaining

> **More contemporary models of emotional functioning have attempted to take into account the influence of affective processing and its underlying neural systems in trying to understand how such information is expressed and processed.**

to variability in social-behavioral functioning are addressed, particularly with respect to problems related to affective disorders and behavioral dyscontrol.

For this theory, how one predicts behaviors is related to an understanding of the person attributes, the situation in which they find themselves, and the inter-relationship between the person and the situation. In the instance of a child with a traumatic brain injury, the cognitive features that are displayed following the injury are going to have an impact on a wide variety of social situations. How these factors interact will determine how that child will process the affective information from that situation or interaction. Indeed, Yeates et al. (2007) have proposed a heuristic model integrating the fields of social neuroscience and developmental psychology to facilitate our understanding of social development of children with different types of brain injuries. We will wait to see how empirical evidence for this model emerges over time.

Taken together, it is important for the examiner to have a full understanding of a child's cognitive abilities following an injury, not to mention a full understanding of how functions may change over time during recovery, and then begin to examine how these functions may intersect with that child's particular social mileu. This should be the case for the home, school, community, and informal social arenas.

Family Factors

One of the key psychosocial factors to consider following a brain injury during childhood is the functioning of the family unit (Wade, Taylor, Drotar, Stancin, & Yeates, 1998). It is important to remember that in addition to the physical and cognitive deficits that may be present for the child, the parents and siblings of that child also may be suffering as well. This pain and suffering needs to be understood within the context of the family unit as it may have a significant impact on how that child moves through the recovery process. In all likelihood, the brain injury also will disrupt communication patterns in the home and, perhaps, contribute to a period of disequalibrium in the home environment. How the family adapts to this disequalibrium will contribute, in part, to the degree of stress in the family setting. It also affects how adaptive the family will be immediately following the injury and their use of adaptive coping strategies (and maladaptive or ineffective strategies) as the child moves through recovery.

> **Those working with the child following a brain injury should be sensitive to the myriad of family issues that will contribute to the psychosocial environment for that child.**

Finally, it is important to note that during the recovery process, the adaptations of the family may change, with their adaptive capabilities waxing and waning as the child moves through the various stages of recovery. These adaptive capabilities may be further complicated by waves of guilt over failure to prevent the injury that many parents experience following a brain injury to their child. Those working with the child following a brain injury should be sensitive to the myriad of family issues that can contribute to the psychosocial environment for that child.

Findings in children and adolescents with brain injury

Psychiatric Disorders

In addition to the emotional-behavioral dysregulation problems that can be associated with frontal lobe injuries, there are a variety of neuropsychiatric and psychosocial difficulties that can emerge following a traumatic brain injury (Kapapa et al., 2010; Rosema, Crowe, & Anderson, 2012). In addition to newly emergent psychiatric disorders and personality changes evolving post injury (Max et al., 2000), social problem solving (Janusz et al., 2002), dissociation with friends and difficulties making new friends (Prigatano &

Saurabh, 2006), and overall social participation (Bedell & Dumas, 2004) surface as new challenges for these children and their families. Further, social-behavioral functions do not occur in isolation and clearly are affected by disruption to neurocognitive processes (e.g., executive functions) as well as environmental influences (Ganesalingam, Sanson, Anderson, & Yeates, 2007; Muscara et al., 2008; Wells, Minnes, & Phillips, 2009). These factors will need to be taken into account in any assessment of the psychiatric and social-behavioral functioning of a child following a brain injury.

Indeed, it is well known that children sustaining a traumatic brain injury can evidence new psychiatric disorders as well as experience exacerbations of premorbid psychiatric conditions. These types of problems can persist for years beyond the time of injury, particularly for children sustaining more severe injuries and/or sustaining the injury at any earlier chronological age (Karver et al., 2012). Such findings were noted approximately 40 years ago, with Klonoff and Paris (1974) describing denial of injury, lack of concern for the injury, and a deteriorating self-concept in their pediatric sample post injury. These types of social-emotional difficulties have been documented even in children sustaining a mild brain injury (Case et al., 1986), but they tend to be more prevalent in children with moderate to severe brain injuries.

In this regard, Brown, Chadwick, Shaffer, Rutter, and Traub (1981) found that their sample of children who sustained a severe closed head injury showed more than twice the rate of new psychiatric disorders at 4, 12, and 30 months post injury than a group of children with orthopedic injuries below the brain stem and typically developing controls. In these instances, a wide range of psychiatric disorders was represented, including excessive social disinhibitory behaviors; however, over time, many of the diagnoses tended to be internalizing in nature (e.g., increased depression, anxiety). More recent investigations have demonstrated heightened rates of Attention Deficit/Hyperactivity Disorder (Bloom et al., 2001), new onset anxiety disorders (Luis & Mittenberg, 2002), and depressive symptoms (Kirkwood et al., 2000). When the externalizing types of behaviors persist, they do appear to be more resistant to treatment efforts and less likely to resolve over time (Bloom et al., 2001).

The rates of poor social adjustment difficulties—that were not present pre-injury—arising from severe TBI in children have ranged from 60% to 76% at one year post injury (Bloom et al., 2001; Lehmkuhl & Thoma, 1990; Max et al., 1998); 36% at two years post injury; 50% at three years post injury (Filley et al., 1987); 36% at four years post injury (Max et al., 1997; Schwartz et al., 2003); and 50% at five years post injury (Klonoff et al., 1977). Additionally, Fletcher, Ewing-Cobbs, Miner, Levin, and Eisenberg (1990), and Max et al. (1998) reported that their sample of children with severe brain injuries showed significant declines in their adaptive behaviors at one year post injury, along with less social and school involvement, when compared to children sustaining milder brain injuries.

Yeates and Taylor (2006) also documented the extension of these problems into the school setting. These investigators showed that their sample of children with severe traumatic brain injury experienced significantly higher rates of emotional and behavioral problems than a comparison group of children who sustained brain injuries of a moderate degree of severity and those with only orthopedic injuries. In addition, these findings remained stable at the four year follow-up time point. Yeates and Taylor (2006) noted that these behavioral difficulties

> **Indeed, it is well known that children sustaining a traumatic brain injury can evidence new psychiatric disorders as well as experience exacerbations of premorbid psychiatric conditions.**

were predictive of poorer classroom performance and a greater likelihood that a child would be receiving some type of special education intervention, and that long-term outcomes could be accounted for by the integrity of executive functions, pragmatic language, and social problem solving (Yeates et al., 2004)

Relatedly, although it may not be a major issue for children, particularly those in a family situation, the issue of increased substance abuse requires mention, especially with respect to older adolescents. It is important to note that the relationship between traumatic brain injury and substance abuse is a two-way street. This inter-relationship is based on the knowledge that approximately 50% of traumatic brain injuries in adults are related to the use of alcohol and other substances and, in fact, about two-thirds of survivors admit to a substance abuse problem that was present prior to the brain injury. Further, approximately one-third of adult substance abusers described having at least one head injury with an associated loss of consciousness. Post injury, approximately 20% of adults may be vulnerable to developing a substance abuse disorder.

The linkage of these findings to the adolescent population should not be minimized following a brain injury, and it will be important for this aspect to be included as part of a larger assessment following a traumatic brain injury. For adolescents, the presence of a substance abuse disorder not only can interfere with learning, social relationships, and other daily activities, but it also is known to slow the recovery process and likely hinder transition into age-appropriate activities of young adulthood. Consequently, questions related to substance use, and risk for such behaviors, always should be included in any assessment of traumatic brain injury, particularly for adolescents.

> **Consequently, questions related to substance use, and risk for such behaviors, always should be included in any assessment of traumatic brain injury, particularly for adolescents.**

Neuroaffective Processing

Despite the evidence showing that children will manifest social-behavioral difficulties following a moderate to severe brain injury (Yeates et al., 2007; Yeates et al., 2009), to date there has been relatively little work examining the emotional processing capabilities of children following a brain injury. While the adult literature has demonstrated that survivors will show deficits following an injury in emotional recognition (Bornhofen & McDonald, 2008), identification of facial emotions (Letswaart, Carwford, & Currie., 2008), and understanding emotional prosody (Milders, Fuchs, & Crawford, 2003), few studies have examined the issue of emotional processing in children after a brain injury. What data are available do suggest that children sustaining a brain injury, typically moderate to severe injuries, will evidence problems with emotional recognition and understanding of affect across modalities (Tonks, Williams, Framptom, Yates, & Slater, 2007; Turkstra et al., 2001). Further, while many of these emotional processing deficits have been linked to the neurocognitive deficits that can be present following a brain injury, Tonks et al. (2007) have demonstrated that these deficits can be dissociated from the cognitive impairments. Most recently, Schmidt et al. (2010) provided evidence for the presence of deficits in emotional prosody and facial emotional recognition in children following moderate to severe closed head injuries when compared to an orthopedically impaired comparison group without brain injuries. Additionally, these investigators noted the importance of higher socioeconomic status and younger age at the time of injury as critical contributors to a more rapid rate of recovery of these emotional processing functions over a two year time period.

Similarly, efforts over the past decade have been directed to the presence of theory of mind (i.e., the ability to understand the mental states and intentions of others in order to expect what other people know and what actions they might take) in children following a TBI. In one of the first studies to address this issue, Turkstra, Dixon, and Baker (2004) reported that their sample of adolescents experienced greater difficulty with theory of mind tasks when compared to typically developing peers, with the group differences increasing with more complex theory of mind tasks. A similar finding was reported by Watz, Yeates, Taylor, Stancin, and Wade (2009) in preschool children with TBI using a first-order theory of mind task, with the findings being most pronounced in the severe TBI group. These investigators (Walz, Yeates, Taylor, Stancin, & Wade, 2010) also showed first-order and second-order theory of mind impairments persisting for at least one year post-injury when compared to their age-matched typically developing peers and an Orthopedically Impaired comparison group. These findings were replicated most recently by Dennis et al. (2012). Dennis, Agostino, Roncadin, and Levin (2009) noted that the manifestation of theory of mind in children following a TBI appears to be dependent on a number of neurocognitive abilities, such as working memory and inhibitory control, in order to function adequately.

Family Functions

As noted above, the potential for family dysfunction is present in nearly all families following an injury to their child. As might be surmised, the number and severity of the issues confronted by a family will be mediated, in large part, by the severity of the brain injury. Families where there is a child with a mild, or perhaps a moderate injury may experience less stress, and this stress may last for a shorter amount of time than a family who has a child who sustained a severe brain injury.

Interestingly, the functioning of the family unit prior to a brain injury appears to be a better predictor of how that family will be functioning one year post injury than the severity of the brain injury. Specifically, families showing more cohesion, less stress, and better communication following an injury tend to adapt better than families who have problems in these areas prior to the injury, with these findings persisting at least three years post-injury (Rivara et al., 1996). In turn, their children tend to have fewer social-behavioral difficulties and better academic skills one year post-injury.

Further, Anderson, Catroppa, Haritou, Morse, and Rosenfeld (2005) found that the feelings of burden experienced by a family unit were accounted for by severity of injury, the degree of functional difficulties, and the presence of behavioral problems for as much as 30 months post-injury; however, the functioning of the family prior to the injury was a strong predictor of family functioning at the 30 month follow-up point. Rivara et al. (1996) noted that equilibrium in the family unit is achieved only when the overall stress levels are reduced and new, but different coping mechanisms are established by the family members.

These adaptations tend to be major traits of families who appear to be more resilient. Stancin, Wade, Walz, Yeates, and Taylor (2008) noted that the initial impact on the family's ability to adapt following the TBI was influenced by the presence of chronic life stressors, family resources, and parent distress, with these general findings being present 18 months post-injury in children injured during the preschool years (Wade, Walz, Yeates, & Taylor, 2010). The nature of parent response to the injury (e.g., warmth versus negativity) also appears to have a significant impact on the family's ability to adapt following an injury (Wade, Walz, Taylor, Stancin, & Yeates, 2011). Despite these findings, Wade et al. (2006) have demonstrated the long-term struggles of families to adapt in a satisfactory manner up to six years post-injury.

Siblings within a family where another child has sustained a TBI also can be affected in a unique fashion. Swift et al. (2003) showed an increased rate of negative sibling relationships in these families, particularly for mixed gender sibling pairs, and behavioral problems in children with TBI contributed to these relationship problems as well as an increased rate of behavior problems in the unaffected sibling.

Table 11.1 Examples of Social-Behavioral-Emotional Assessment Techniques.

Behavioral Observations
Applied Behavior Analysis/Task Analysis
Behavior Assessment System for Children-2 Behavior Observation System
Clinical Interviews
Unstructured Clinical Interview
Kiddie Schedule for Affective Disorders and Schizophrenia - Present and Life Time Version
Diagnostic Inventory Schedule for Children
Structured Clinical Interview for DSM Disorders
Child and Adolescent Psychiatric Assessment
Diagnostic Interview for Children and Adolescents-Revised
Semi-Structured Interview for Children and Adolescents
Preschool Age Psychiatric Assessment
Vineland Adaptive Behavior Scale-2
Behavioral Rating Scales-Global
Behavioral Assessment System for Children-2
Conner's Rating Scales
Child Behavior Checklist
Child Symptom Inventory
Devereux Scales of Mental Disorders
Behavioral Rating Scales-Specific
State-Trait Anger Expression Inventory
Childhood Depression Inventory-2

A review of this literature (Sambuco, Brookes, & Lah, 2008) indicated that the siblings of children who sustained a severe TBI and who have ongoing psychiatric issues are at-risk for negative psychosocial outcomes and negative, unexpected changes in their lives. Additional longitudinal studies should shed light on this important topic; moreover, from an assessment perspective, it will be important for this aspect of the family to receive close scrutiny.

Finally, a related psychosocial issue pertains to the quality of life of the child and family following a TBI. Emergent data have begun to document problems in the broad area of quality of life in children who have sustained a severe traumatic brain injury (Horneman, Folkesson, Sintonen, von Wendt, & Emanuelson, 2005; Kapapa et al., 2010; McCarthy et al., 2006; Souza, Braga, Filho, & Dellatolas, 2007; Stancin et al., 2002; Tilford et al., 2007). Using a large sample of children with traumatic brain injury, McCarthy et al. (2006) found 42% reported health related quality of life impairments at three months post injury. These impairments were described across multiple dimensions for children who sustained moderate and severe brain injuries, and the impairments persisted over time. In fact, recent follow-up reports have documented health related quality of life impairments in children who have sustained a severe traumatic brain injury from one year to decades post injury (Anderson, Brown, Newitt, & Hoile, 2011; Erickson, Montague, & Gerstle, 2010; Limond, Dorris, & McMillan, 2009).

For children with mild to moderate traumatic brain injuries, quality of life difficulties appear to lessen over time, with few problems being described beyond 12 months post injury (Anderson et al., 2011; Petersen, Scherwath, Fink, & Koch, 2008); however, this will require further study (Limond et al., 2009), particularly with respect to how quality of life interacts with both injury (e.g., severity) and non-injury related contributors (e.g.,

Table 11.1 (continued) Examples of Social-Behavioral-Emotional Assessment Techniques.

Behavioral Rating Scales-Specific
State-Trait Anger Expression Inventory
Childhood Depression Inventory-2
Revised Children's Manifest Anxiety Scale-2
Young Mania Rating Scale
Yale-Brown Obsessive-Compulsive Scale
Alcohol Use Disorders Identification Test
Brief Psychiatric Rating Scale
Social Skills Rating Scale
ADHD Rating Scale
Coping Inventory
Reynolds Child Depression Scale-2/Reynolds Adolescent Depression Scale-2
Pediatric Quality of Life Scale
Neuroaffective Measures
Diagnostic Analysis of Nonverbal Accuracy
Cambridge Neuropsychological Test Automated Battery Affective Go No-Go Task
Benton Facial Recognition Test
NEPSY-II Social Perception Domain
Penn Emotional Recognition Task
The Awareness of Social Inference Test
Reading the Mind in the Eyes Test
Family Measures
Family Adaptability and Cohesion Evaluation Scale-IV
Family Assessment Measure III
McMaster Family Assessment Device-III

Assessment Procedures

The assessment procedures for measuring social-behavioral and affective functioning in children following a brain injury are quite varied, but offer a wide range of possibilities when working with a child post-injury. In fact, there is such a large number of assessment procedures and techniques that it is beyond the scope of this volume to touch on all of them; however, within the psychiatric and behavioral realm, there are several major options available to the clinician. These include good, old fashion behavioral observations, unstructured and structured clinical interviews, and various global and specific rating scales. A sampling of these types of tools are provided in Table 11.1.

Behavioral Observations

The simplicity of basic structured observations should not cloud their potential utility when working with children following a brain injury. Indeed, these types of assessment strategies have extraordinary flexibility and will be applicable to children showing all types of social and behavioral difficulties.

Behavioral observations represent one of the key components of applied behavior analysis (ABA). ABA requires operationally defined goals and objectives that, ultimately, lead to a detailed treatment program and a specific progress monitoring plan. It also is a core component of a Functional Behavioral Analysis, a set of procedures that are conducted in most schools related to behavioral concerns, and that typically occur in the child's natural ecology.

premorbid family functioning, socioeconomic status) over time. In this regard, Anderson, Brown, and Newitt (2010) found that 83% of their adult survivors of a childhood TBI reported their quality of life to be satisfactory, with poor quality of life being related to lower levels of independence, severity of the injury, a younger age at the time of injury, lack of a high school education, and ongoing social-behavioral difficulties.

In general, a behavioral observation will provide detailed information related to why a behavior occurs, particularly with respect to its antecedents and consequences, as well as to its frequency, duration, and intensity. Consequently, this type of appraisal should lead to modifying the conditions that either support or hinder the appearance of a more adaptive behavior for that child. Ongoing measurement of the target behavior is a critical component of ABA and it all begins with the behavioral observations. A number of resources are available to the examiner or clinician, such as the BASC-2 Behavioral Observation System, with other selected assessment resources being devoted exclusively to children with brain injuries (e.g., Bruce et al., 2006).

Clinical Interviews

Nearly all clinicians are trained to perform clinical interviews. These are as varied as the professionals who conduct them, the training programs from which they come, and the idiosyncratic nuances of the professionals themselves. The unstructured clinical interviews provide an enormous amount of information on the medical background, developmental history, school functioning, pharmacology, family history, and the presenting problems of that particular child. They also allow a free flowing interaction to occur between the clinician and the child and/or family. With respect to behavior or psychiatric problems following a brain injury, such an approach can be the precursor to detailed behavioral observations as noted above, and it can contribute to specific diagnostic information related to the presence or emergence of a significant psychiatric disorder.

In contrast, the structured or semi-structured clinical interview provides a mechanism to ensure that all of the necessary clinical questions are asked, with appropriate follow-up questions being raised as necessary. It is a measurement tool that assists professionals in making an accurate clinical diagnosis. Much in the same spirit as many of the tests mentioned in this book, the semi-structured clinical interview contains questions that are standardized, thus everyone receives the same modules or questions. In general, these questions typically ask about the appearance of specific symptoms, their presentation, duration, and severity.

This type of approach is a bit more rigid in its application, but has the advantage of ensuring that all necessary questions are asked, particularly with respect to presenting problematic symptoms or worries. These types of semi-structured interviews also tend to be intimately linked to psychiatric nomenclature such that a diagnosis can be asserted once completed.

There are a number of semi-structured clinical interviews available to the clinician including the Kiddie-Schedule for Affective Disorders and Schizophrenia Present and Lifetime Version (K-SADS-PL), Diagnostic Interview Schedule for Children (DISC), Structured Clinical Interview for DSM Disorders (SCID) and its variants (Kid-SCID), the Child and Adolescent Psychiatric Assessment (CAPA), Diagnostic Interview for Children and Adolescents-Revised (DICA-R), and the Semi-Structured Interview for Children and Adolescents. In each of these semi-structured interviews, the parent and child are typically interviewed separately over the course of 1 to 2 hours each. For example, the K-SADS-PL is applicable for children, ages 6-18, and provides questions addressing most psychiatric symptoms, with a summary diagnosis (or diagnoses) utilizing all sources of potential information. Examiners have the option of utilizing the entire tool, or selecting targeted modules that reflect the primary concerns of the child.

The K-SADS-PL historically has been employed in the research setting, but one of the more popular semi-structured interviews has made a cross-over into the clinical world: the SCID. The SCID is formatted in both clinical and research versions, with the latter version containing more questions that pertain to an increased number of psychiatric disorders. Similar to the format for the K-SADS-PL, the SCID permits the interviewer to select specific modules to administer to the parent and child, with 10 different modules from which to choose (e.g., mood disorders, substance use disorders, anxiety disorders).

A third example, the Semi-Structured Interview for Children and Adolescents (McConaughy & Achenbach, 2001), is another tool by which a clinician can gain specific behavioral and psychiatric diagnostic information from a child. This semi-structured interview was designed to be administered directly to the child, ages 6 to 18, and requires approximately 75 minutes. In line with the dimensional classification approach that underlies the format of the Child Behavior Checklist, this semi-structured interview yields eight syndrome scales including Aggressive Behavior, Anxious, Anxious/Depressed, Attention Problems, Family Problems, Resistant, Strange, Withdrawn, three summary scales (i.e., Internalizing, Externalizing, Total Problems), and a number of DSM-oriented scales.

This type of assessment methodology even has been applied to very young children in the form of the Preschool Age Psychiatric Assessment (PAPA). The PAPA is the downward extension of the CAPA and is a semi-structured interview completed by parents of children ages 2 through 5 years. Similar to its older children counterpart, the PAPA is based on the DSM-IV and provides a summary diagnosis based on the symptoms described. This may be a particularly useful tool for preschool children who have sustained a brain injury, particularly from the perspective that in many instances cognitive and behavioral deficits can lie "silent" until later in life when such deficits are challenged. Obtaining this type of information during the preschool years could permit examination of subtle, emergent symptoms that may later manifest into larger social-behavioral challenges and difficulties.

Finally, although not specifically devoted to psychopathology and associated behavioral-emotional difficulties, the semi-structured interview format has been extended to obtain information pertaining to adaptive behavior. This may be critical following a brain injury and may serve to provide specific programming pertaining to areas such as social skills, communication, and activities of daily living. The Vineland Adaptive Behavior Scale-2 (VABS-2) is one of the most widely used measures of adaptive behavior. The VABS provides for a comprehensive measure of adaptive functioning, including parsing out broad domains of functioning into specific behaviors that should facilitate more targeted interventions. A maladaptive behavior scale also can be administered via the semi-structured interview format. The VABS can be used from infancy through young adulthood, provides age-based standard scores, and is available in a rating scale format for the parent or guardian to complete; however, for those working with very young children, the semi-structured interview actually provides more items at the lower levels than the questionnaire, and this may be critical in the evaluation and developmental monitoring of an infant, toddler, or preschooler following a brain injury.

It should be noted, however, that the structured clinical interviews do require significant amounts of training and practice so as to obtain adequate reliability in obtaining the necessary clinical information. They also require a strong knowledge base in childhood psychopathology. This will ensure that they will be administered in the required standardized manner and facilitate the attainment of an accurate diagnosis, thus minimizing false positives and false negatives. This is especially critical in the instance of pediatric brain injury where various clinical features can manifest in children following a traumatic brain injury (e.g., heightened somatic symptoms), and it will be important for these features not to be confused with manifest psychopathology. Undoubtedly, the routine crossover of these types of assessment strategies into the clinical realm has been slowed by these demands.

Behavioral Rating Scales

There is a long list of behavioral ratings scales that are available to the clinician and, as noted earlier, this list is too lengthy to explicate in this volume. In fact, one probably can find a rating scale for any targeted behavioral problem. In general, though, behavior rating scales typically can be subdivided into two kinds: global and specific. The use of a global rating scale versus a specific rating scale is not mutually exclusive as both may be selected to address a particular set of challenging behaviors or emotional problems, and this should be useful when working with a pediatric brain injury population.

For the global types of rating scales, there are a number from which to choose that include the Behavioral Assessment System for Children-2 (BASC-2), Conner's Rating Scale (CRS), Child Behavior Checklist (CBCL), the Child Symptom Inventory (CSI), and the Devereux Scales of Mental Disorders. All of these global rating scales are well normed, standardized, and address assessment from a multi-rater (typically parents and teachers), multi-setting (typically home and school settings), multi-instrument (targeted items for parents, teachers, and children allow for somewhat different questions to be asked of each respondent) design. In the instance of the Child Symptom Inventory and the Child Behavior Checklist, DSM-IV diagnostic analogs also can be produced along with age-based standard scores. The age range for these tools is quite large, ranging generally from early preschool through young adulthood, which should permit longitudinal tracking of social-behavioral issues throughout the recovery process. Selected examples of these tools are listed in Table 11.1.

Like the global rating scales, there is a wide range and number of specific behavior rating scales. One can probably find a specific rating scale for any targeted behavior of interest. Following a brain injury, there may be any number of behavioral symptoms that could manifest but, typically, problems with aggression and mood regulation will be most prevalent. In that regard, scales such as the State-Trait Anger Expression Inventory, Childhood Depression Inventory-2, Revised Children's Manifest Anxiety Scale-2, Young Mania Rating Scale, Yale-Brown Obsessive-Compulsive Scale, Alcohol Use Disorders Identification Test, Brief Psychiatric Rating Scale, Social Skills Rating Scale, ADHD Rating Scale, and the Coping Inventory are only a few of the tools available to clinicians.

For example, following a brain injury, a child may begin to experience depression either directly related to the injury or perhaps in a secondary fashion given the loss of friends, a changing social scene, and/or an inability to return to previously enjoyed or accomplished activities. In addition to information on depressive symptoms that can be obtained from the global rating scales, the Child Depression Inventory-2 is a well normed and standardized rating scale that is quick and relatively easy to use. It contains 28 items pertaining to various aspects of depression for children ages 7 to 17. The CDI-2 yields age-based scores pertaining to the presence of emotional problems and functional problems, with specific subscales being provided for negative mood/physical symptoms, negative self-esteem, interpersonal problems, and ineffectiveness. Similarly, the Revised Children's Manifest Anxiety Scale-2 provides a parallel set of indices that pertain to anxiety symptoms. This rating scale is designed for children 6 though 19 years of age and requires about 10 to 15 minutes of the child's time to complete. The test yields an age-based Total Anxiety Score along with four subscales: Physiological Anxiety, Worry, Social Anxiety, and Defensiveness. A validity index also is generated (Inconsistent Responding Index).

Finally, it will be important to assess the child's quality of life following a brain injury. One measure that is available to clinicians is the Pediatric Quality of Life Scale (PedsQL; Varni, 2012). The PedsQL has a long-standing research history that has demonstrated its support across a wide range of conditions and chronic illnesses. The PedsQL is a brief, 23-item rating scale that asks parents, teachers, and children (depending on their age) specific questions about that child's health-related quality of life across several key dimensions: Physical Functioning, Emotional Functioning, Psychosocial Functioning, Social Functioning, and School Functioning. Three summary scales also are calculated: Physical Health, Psychosocial, and Total Summary. The PedsQL typically requires approximately 5 minutes to complete, and children can complete their version starting at 8 years of age. Versions of the PedsQL can be used with children as young as 24 months of age up through young

> **In general, though, behavior rating scales typically can be subdivided into two kinds: global and specific.**

adulthood. Specific modules also are available for various disorders (e.g., diabetes). Although brain injury is not yet one of targeted modules, the general quality of life items provided in the PedsQL should yield critical information as to a child's quality of life following a brain injury as well as assist in tracking these issues through the recovery process.

Neuroaffective Measures

Several of these types of measures were mentioned in Chapter 10 in the discussion of the ventromedial prefrontal cortex and associated brain functions (e.g., DANVA; CANTAB Affective Go No-Go Task). These types of tasks are not readily available in the clinical domain in large part because many of them are currently being developed and employed in experimental neuroscience research studies (e.g., morphing faces in the study of autism spectrum disorders). Precursors to these types of measures, such as the Benton Facial Recognition Test, provide information pertaining to a child's ability to recognition faces across different contexts, remain important in the assessment process given the appearance of conditions such as prosopagnosia (i.e., face regognition impairment) following many mild to moderate injuries.

There also are tasks, such as those comprising the NEPSY-II Social Perception Domain, which provide measures of Theory of Mind and Affect Recognition. These types of tasks begin to approximate some of the neuroaffective measures via the vehicle of social cognition. On the NEPSY-II subtests, the child is asked to recognize different emotions (Affective Recognition) and to guess what another person is thinking and feeling (Theory of Mind). It is expected that more of these types of tools will become available as tasks move from the research laboratories into the clinical setting in the next decade.

Family Measures

The assessment of family functioning following a traumatic brain injury is not only critical to the recovery of the child, but also consistent with the concept of the long-held notion of conducting interventions within the context of the family unit (Sroufe & Fleeson, 1986). In general, family measures have been designed to assess cohesion, communication, support systems, and other types of relationships within the family unit. Additionally, there are well over a thousand tools that have been developed or made available for use in measuring these various nuances of the family system (see *Handbook of Family Measurement Techniques*, Touliatos, Perlmutter, & Straus, 2001; Carlson, 2003). Within the realm of pediatric brain injury, several of these tools have been employed including the Family Adaptability and Cohesion Evaluation Scale-IV (FACES-IV), Family Assessment Measure III (FAM-III), and the McMaster Family Assessment Device-III (FAD-III).

For example, the FACES-IV (Olson, 2011) evolved from family theory and zeroed in on two major dimensions of the family: cohesion and adaptability. Items tapping into these dimensions provide an examination of relationship boundaries, closeness, and coalitions; decision-making, family power, and role relationships; and negotiation style. The FACES is a Likert-type scale with 30 items, with available normative data, and yields a cohesion score and an adaptability score.

Similarly, the McMaster FAD-III (Epstein & Bishop, 1993; Skinner, Santa-Barbara, & Steinhauer, 1983) provides an assessment of family functioning across three key areas: overall family health, dyadic relationships, and individual relationships within the family unit. This tool allows for a multirater format and a multigenerational appraisal of the family's functioning that provides scores for six different family domains: Task Accomplishment, Communication/Affective Expression, Role Performance, Affective Involvement, Control, and Values and Norms. It also has been translated into 14 different languages, which should facilitate multicultural assessment needs.

For children who have sustained a brain injury, family functioning will be one critical variable in how well they recover and adjust to any life changes that may have occurred; consequently, it will be important for the clinician to obtain an appraisal of the family functioning, and to provide ongoing assessment of the family system as the child moves through the various phases of recovery.

Summary

Although the physical and/or cognitive disabilities following a brain injury are most apparent, the social, emotional, and behavioral difficulties that can arise likely are the most troublesome to families, teachers, and employers throughout the process of recovery and in terms of long-term residual challenges for that individual. This chapter has focused on a number of different approaches to the assessment of the social, emotional, and behavioral challenges including behavioral observations, clinical interviews, and various kinds of rating scales.

In addition, it is important to reiterate that these types of problems do not occur in a vacuum. Their interaction with specific settings, different people, and different developmental time points will remain a critical aspect to the assessment as well. The various conditions and situations under which behaviors manifest may dictate the duration, frequency, and severity of the problem, and they may implicate different types of intervention strategies. Consequently, a multi-rater, multi-setting, multi-instrument design is suggested whenever possible.

The assessment of these complex social, behavioral, and emotional manifestations following an injury in childhood will be as important as the cognitive and physical assessments that should occur. Indeed, the findings from social-behavioral assessments may not only lay the foundation for the types of intervention that may be necessary in the present, but they also may be important with respect to future strategies for behavior management. For example, it is not uncommon for social and behavioral difficulties "to lay silent" until a later developmental time point—in large part due to damage to the brain that will disrupt neurodevelopmental processes and, consequently, later functions. Having some indication of precursors to this may lessen the impact of their appearance much later in time. Also, given the potential increasing prevalence of emotional and behavioral disorders over the course of recovery, it would seem that using these tools as monitoring devices will be critical to their application in pediatric brain injury.

Finally, it is suggested that clinicians not overlook subthreshold signs and symptoms of potentially emergent problems that will interact with cognitive deficits in complicated, but in many instances, unknown ways.

> **In general, family measures have been designed to assess cohesion, communication, support systems, and other types of relationships within the family unit.**

Chapter 12
Child Neuropsychological Batteries

Description

Up to this point, you have been exposed to an assessment approach to brain injury in children and adolescents that takes into account various brain functions and their associated components. These functions and their components are the basis for instrument selection in a flexible battery approach as noted in Chapter 3. Additionally, the flexible battery approach has overtaken the fixed battery approach to assessment in terms of its frequency and popularity of use (Rabin et al., 2005). Despite this trend, however, there are a number of neuropsychological batteries for children that provide a broad assessment of various brain functions in a reliable fashion. Although not all of these batteries are "fixed," they clearly offer an alternative to conducting an assessment using multiple tests. In that regard, child neuropsychological batteries, like many of the other batteries mentioned in this volume, offer a key advantage of having all of the tasks being standardized on the same sample, thus minimizing the error that can occur when different tests are used that have different normative pools.

Although the focus of this text has been on the flexible battery approach, the astute clinician will become familiar with the available batteries and their features, and subsequently will utilize them as necessary for a particular child or adolescent. For example, if a child who has sustained a brain injury already has been assessed with one of these neuropsychological batteries, it may be in the best interest of neurodevelopmental surveillance and monitoring to utilize the same set of procedures as this strategy may provide the best tracking mechanism for determining stability, decline, or progress during the recovery period. The use of a neuropsychological battery also may provide a more convenient way to conduct an assessment at bedside or under other conditions where a large number of tests simply cannot be transported.

Table 12.1 Traditional and Computerized Neuropsychological Batteries for Children and Adolescents.

Traditional Neuropsychological Batteries for Children and Adolescents
Reitan-Indiana Neuropsychological Battery (ages 5 to 8)
Halstead-Reitan Neuropsychological Battery for Older Children (ages 9 to 14)
Halstead-Reitan Neuropsychological Battery (ages 15 and above)
Luria-Nebraska Neuropsychological Battery-Children's Revision (ages 5 to 12)
Luria-Nebraska Neuropsychological Battery (ages 13 and above)
Woodcock-Johnson-III Cognitive Battery (ages 2 and above)
NEPSY-II (ages 3 to 16)
Dean-Woodcock Neuropsychological Battery
Neuropsychological Assessment Battery (ages 18 and above)
Wechsler Intelligence Scale for Children-IV-Integrated
Computerized Neuropsychological Batteries for Children and Adolescents
Cambridge Neuropsychological Automated Battery (ages 4 and above)
Penn Neuropsychological Battery (ages 18 and above)
CNS Vital Signs Computerized Neuropsychological Test Battery (ages 7 and above)
Automated Neuropsychological Assessment Metrics (ages 18 and above)
Immediate Post Concussion Assessment and Cognitive Testing (ages 11 and above)

Assessment Procedures

When one considers the number of neuropsychological batteries that are available, there are several choices that span both traditional batteries as well as computerized batteries. The computerized assessment batteries have been more recent in origin, but have proven to be formidable in their use, particularly in research studies and pharmacological drug trials. In both instances, though, the batteries are designed to cover a broad range of brain-based constructs with a predetermined set of tasks. Additionally, as noted in Chapter 3, these batteries have the advantage of replicability across situations and across time for a specific individual. Examples of the traditional and computerized batteries can be seen in Table 12.1.

Traditional Child Neuropsychological Batteries

Traditional paper-and-pencil neuropsychological batteries typically have been constructed based on adult instruments and assessment strategies, but with some developmental constraints being asserted. These constraints usually have included fewer tasks, shortened tasks, and less complex tasks, with more recent approaches trying to be sensitive to infant, toddler, and preschooler development (e.g., Heffelfinger & Koop, 2009). Normative data also were included as an adjustment for child capabilities, but neurodevelopmental considerations were not necessarily a driving force in the development and formation of these earlier batteries. To date, there are a number of neuropsychological batteries from which to choose, with age range, psychometric properties, and flexibility being key variables for consideration.

Of all of the available child neuropsychological batteries, perhaps the Halstead-Reitan Neuropsychological Batteries hold the most reverence within the field. Although the popularity and subsequent usage of these tools have declined over the years, many of the original Halstead-Reitan tasks remain staples of American neuropsychological assessment at both the child and adult levels (e.g., Trail-Making Test, Finger Oscillation). From a historical perspective, Reitan took the teachings of Halstead and further refined a set of assessment procedures that was comprehensive, sensitive to both focal and diffuse brain injuries, and for its time, psychometrically reliable and valid. In its present day form, there are three batteries that have arisen from this earlier work: the Reitan-Indiana Neuropsychological Battery for children 5 through 8 years of age; the Halstead-Reitan Neuropsychological Battery for Older Children ages 9 through 14; and the Halstead-Reitan Neuropsychological Battery for ages 15 years and above.

For example, the Halstead-Reitan Neuropsychological Battery for Older Children contained 13 different tasks that assess lateral dominance (Lateral Dominance Examination), gross motor strength (Grip Strength in both hands), sensory-perceptual functions (Sensory-Perceptual Examination), fine-motor speed and control (Finger Oscillation), basic language including speech sounds (Aphasia Screening Test, Speech Sounds Perception Test), attention (Seashore Rhythm Test), higher-order tactile functions (Tactile Performance Test), set shifting (Trail-Making Test), and concept formation (Category Test). Results from these tasks were normatively based and examined for the level of functioning, the pattern of functioning, left/right differences, and the presence of pathognomonic signs. The age-appropriate Wechsler intelligence scale also was administered as part of this battery of tasks. Many of the tasks remain critical in the assessment of children following a brain injury and, indeed, some of the initial neuropsychological findings on pediatric brain injuries were uncovered using the Reitan batteries (e.g., Boll, 1983).

A second battery designed for children was the Luria-Nebraska Neuropsychological Battery-Children's Revision (Golden, 1981). This battery used Lurian theory (Luria, 1980) as its core foundation and evolved Luria's bedside tasks into a standardized approach to assessment. Similar to the development of the versions of the Halstead-Reitan Battery for younger children, this version of the Luria-Nebraska was a downward extension of the version for older individuals. In addition, Golden made an effort to include Luria's neurodevelopmental theory in the construction of the assessment tasks. This battery was comprised of key constructs and included items measuring: Motor, Rhythm, Tactile, Visual, Receptive Speech, Expressive Language, Writing, Reading, Arithmetic, Memory, and Intelligence. Additionally, the Luria-Nebraska Children's Revision yielded a norm-based examination of level of performance and pattern of performance, as well as scales addressing the presence of left/right differences and pathognomonic signs. In parallel with the findings on pediatric brain injuries from the Halstead-Reitan Batteries, work with this version of the Luria-Nebraska showed children with various documented brain injuries to perform more poorly than controls (Gustavson et al., 1984).

Despite the initial success and historical imprint of these two traditional neuropsychological batteries, contemporary efforts to create neuropsychological batteries for children and adolescents have been more sophisticated in their derivation and conceptualization. Batteries such as the Dean-Woodcock Neuropsychological Battery, the Woodcock-Johnson III Cognitive Battery, Cognitive Assessment System, the Wechsler Intelligence Scale for Children-IV Integrated, and the Neuropsychological Assessment Battery all have had a significant impact on the field and have afforded clinicians a range of batteries from which to choose. In addition, the more contemporary batteries are built on evolving neuroscience findings pertaining to brain functioning, underlying neural systems, and advanced methodologies. For example, the Woodcock-Johnson III Cognitive Battery is derived from the Cattell-Horn-Carroll Model of cognitive functioning and entails the use of eight core functions that include comprehension-knowledge, long-term retrieval, visual-spatial thinking, auditory processing, fluid reasoning, processing speed, short-term memory, and quantitative knowledge. The Woodcock-Johnson also provides summary scores related to key brain functions such as phonemic awareness, working memory, broad attention, cognitive fluency, executive processes, and delayed recall. Similarly, the Cognitive Assessment System utilizes the Planning-Attention-Simultaneous-Successive Model (PASS Model) to construct its items and subsequent scales. A strategy assessment checklist also is employed.

> **Despite the initial success and historical imprint of these two traditional neuropsychological batteries, contemporary efforts to create neuropsychological batteries for children and adolescents have been more sophisticated in their derivation and conceptualization.**

In this regard, the NEPSY-II, and its predecessor employed a Lurian model in its approach to pediatric neuropsychological assessment wherein designated brain functions corresponded with selected assessment tasks (Luria, 1966). Although the Halstead-Reitan and Lurian-Nebraska batteries were hailed as having strong normative bases, the NEPSY holds the distinction of being the first well normed and standardized neuropsychological battery for children and adolescents. This distinction is significant given the need for such a tool in the field of child neuropsychology, particularly with the advancing demands for stronger psychometric properties. While other concepts from Lurian Theory, such as functional systems and zones of proximal development, are not clearly articulated with respect to their integration into the NEPSY-II, the domains provided are clearly multidimensional and representative of the broad range of neurocognitive functions espoused by most neuropsychological models (Hooper, 2010).

The NEPSY-II includes the domains of Attention and Executive Functioning, Language, Memory and Learning, Sensorimotor, and Visuospatial Processing. The NEPSY-II also includes the new domain of Social Perception. It is important to note that these neuropsychological domains are not empirically derived, or even statistically independent; but, rather, a conceptual grouping of tasks tapping a variety of functions within a larger domain. In that regard, unlike its predecessor, the NEPSY-II does not provide individual domain or composite scores; however, the NEPSY-II offers significant flexibility in administration in that single tasks, multiple tasks within a domain, or the entire battery can be used, depending on the referral questions. The extension of tasks into the middle adolescent years (i.e. up to age 16.9 years) required the addition of new items to a number of subtests (e.g., Arrows, Design Copying), but should serve its users well with respect to having options for neuropsychological testing in this developmental period.

Similarly, the NEPSY-II represents a significant effort to extend neuropsychological testing into the preschool years. Outside of selected intellectual batteries and single test approaches, there are few batteries that have attempted to provide neuropsychological measurement for such a young population. The NEPSY-II should facilitate increased precision with respect to description of neurocognitive functions for a wide variety of children with both neurological and neurodevelopmental disorders and, subsequently, facilitate prescription of specific treatment strategies and interventions. It is important to note that the NEPSY-II has been employed with pediatric traumatic brain injury, with the findings reflecting significant differences on a number of key functions when compared to typically developing controls on a number of key functions (Korkman et al., 2007).

Finally, one of the more creative approaches to traditional child neuropsychological assessment is represented by the Wechsler Intelligence Scale for Children-IV Integrated (WISC-IV-I). This approach is based, in part, on the Boston Process Approach described in Chapter 3. Here, the core battery is founded on the WISC-IV, with modifications occuring for a number of subtests to facilitate responding and/or to test assessment hypotheses. Additionally, there are 16 new optional subtests. Specifically, the WISC-IV-I provides a comprehensive measure of neurocognitive strengths and weaknesses which can be customized for a specific child based on referral questions and/or hypothesis testing by the examiner. In addition to the new subtests, the standard administration of a number of the core subtests is modified to allow for hypothesis testing. For example, within the Verbal Comprehension Index, a multiple choice option is offered for all of the subtests; within the Perceptual Reasoning Index, Block Design is completed using multiple choice of potential visual matches and by adding back the grid lines for all designs; additional subtests are added to the Working Memory Index; and copy and recall conditions are added to the Coding Subtest in the Processing Speed Index. For children with a brain injury, these types of modifications to tasks, and the ability to test limits and engage in hypothesis testing during the assessment process, should promote a more detailed and accurate appraisal of a child's functioning.

Computerized Neuropsychological Batteries for Children

Over the past 20 to 25 years, there has been a slow, but steady growth in the appearance and use of computerized neuropsychological test batteries. This is due, in large part, to the expensive nature of traditional neuropsychological assessment—both in terms of time and cost. In addition, there can be significant human error in the paper-and-pencil tasks, with issues of mobility and flexibility being of concern. By placing many of the paper-and-pencil tasks, or their derivatives, on computer, there is the potential for improved precision and accuracy, increased administration and scoring efficiency, and the inclusion of other measures and alternate forms that may not be as easily obtained with traditional neuropsychological assessment (e.g., reaction time).

With more and more people becoming comfortable with computers, this type of approach may feel more natural for many individuals who have been referred for neuropsychological assessment. Their ease of administration and scoring also contributes to reliability and validity data being collected more easily. Consequently, although these types of approaches have not been universally accepted, or their use widespread, it is likely that they are not going to go away and will become an increasing part of the neuropsychological assessment landscape, especially as tasks are adapted to multi-function cell phones, iPads, and similar technology. For children who have sustained a brain injury, computerized batteries may prove particularly useful in developmental surveillance and ongoing monitoring of recovery and response to various treatments. They have begun to demonstrate their utility in youth and adult return-to-play guidelines that have been adopted by many states across the country. A sampling of these computerized assessments can be seen in Table 12.1.

To date, most of the computerized batteries have been developed for adults, although a number of them are applicable to children. Some of these include the CNS Vital Signs, Computer Administered Neuropsychological Screen, Cambridge Neuropsychological Test Automated Battery, Penn Neuropsychological Battery, MicroCog, NeuroTrax–Mindstreams, Neurobehavioral Evaluation System–3, and Specialty Automated Systems. For example, the Cambridge Neuropsychological Test Automated Battery (CANTAB) is one of the more utilized computerized batteries. Using touch screen technology and a series of language-independent tests, this is also one of the more reliable and valid batteries. The normative base is extensive, with data for young children and geriatric patients, and it is flexible in that clinicians and researchers can form their own specific batteries depending on the referral questions or research questions of interest.

The CANTAB comprises tasks that help train the individual in performing the tests (Motor Screening Test), along with measures of visual memory (Paired Associate Learning, Spatial Recognition Memory), attention (Choice Reaction Time, Simple Reaction Time), executive functions (Attention Switching, Spatial Span, Stockings of Cambridge), semantic/verbal memory (Verbal/Recognition Memory), decision making and response control (Affective Go No-Go, Stop Signal Task), and social cognition (Emotional Recognition Task). These tasks begin at an easy level for most children, but then increase in difficulty as the child completes different aspects of each task. Following a brain injury, a battery of tasks could be constructed that would permit initial assessment of impairments, but also provide a blueprint for monitoring recovery of functioning without overtaxing the stamina of the child.

Another computerized neuropsychological battery that has received some attention, particularly with respect to traumatic brain injuries, is CNS Vital Signs. This computerized neurocognitive battery is built upon several well known neuropsychological procedures and currently is comprised of seven tasks: verbal memory, visual memory, finger tapping, symbol digit coding, the Stroop Test, attentional shifting, and a continuous performance test. The normative sample for this battery ranges from ages 7 to 90 years of age, with validity studies being devoted to individuals with mild cognitive impairment, post-concussion syndrome, and severe traumatic brain injury to mention a few of the comparison groups. Assessment time is relatively quick, with an individual being able to complete all tasks within approximately one hour, and there is an online version that is now available via a web-based application (Gualtieri & Johnson, 2006). The developers of the test are careful to note that this battery should serve as a screening tool and should not be a substitute for formal neuropsychological testing; however, its utility for assessment and monitoring for individuals following a traumatic brain injury holds promise.

Several other computerized tasks, such as CogState Sport, Headminder, Immediate Post-Concussion and Cognitive Testing (ImPACT), and Automated Neuropsychological Assessment Metrics (ANAM), have been developed more explicitly for concussion-related injuries. These assessments typically require anywhere from about 10 to 25 minutes to complete and, because they are computer-based, they can be employed in any number of settings such as athletic events, playgrounds, or even on the battlefield. Additionally, these tests can be used to gain a baseline assessment from an individual prior to a brain injury, and these data are then used to determine recovery of function following a brain trauma. In general, these tests are not comprehensive neuropsychological batteries but, rather, a set of neurocognitive tasks designed to be sensitive to mild brain injuries.

For example, one of the most popular tasks is the Immediate Post-Concussion Assessment and Cognitive Testing (ImPACT; Lovell et al., 2006; Lovell & Maroon, 1990). This computerized battery has evolved to be one of the most used tools at the high school, college, and professional sports levels to determine an athlete's return-to-play after suffering a concussion, and it has been suggested as a standard tool to provide neurocognitive evaluation to all children who are hospitalized with a mild traumatic brain injury (Nance, Polk-Williams, Collins, & Wiebe, 2009). In that regard, it seems that the frequency of concussions is almost at epidemic highs, particularly in the world of sports, and the ImPACT has been one of the key assessment tools to help understand the nature and severity of these injuries. Although the ImPACT should be administered by physicians, athletic trainers, or other licensed healthcare providers who have been trained in its use and also who understand brain injuries, it is important to note that these types of procedures are now being offered at many locations such as sporting good stores. The ImPACT provides a rapid assessment at baseline of several key cognitive functions that are sensitive to the effects of a concussion: attention span, working memory, sustained and selective attention, response variability, nonverbal problem solving, and reaction time.

These tasks form five key summary indices that include: Verbal Memory, Visual Memory, Reaction Time, Impulse Control, and Total Symptoms Composite. A large number of alternate forms can be created so as to facilitate the serial assessment necessary for tracking symptom changes, thus minimizing practice effects. While the administration of the ImPACT is typically conducted in groups of athletes (i.e., 10-15) at baseline, an individual assessment should occur within 24 to 72 hours post-concussion. These findings typically are combined with neurobehavioral assessment of associated concussion symptoms using the ImPACT Symptom Scale wherein 23 post-concussion symptoms are rated on a Likert-scale (Lowell & Collins, 1998). There is now even an application for the ImPACT program on an iPod or iPhone that can assist with the immediate assessment of concussion symptoms as well as an online assessment version.

Summary

As noted earlier in this chapter, the use of neuropsychological batteries has diminished over the years; however, their utility remains important for a number of situations in which neurocognitive assessment following a brain injury is required. The traditional paper-and-pencil approaches clearly have a place in the assessment of children following a brain injury and may serve to address a number of issues that a more flexible battery may not. Similarly, although the "new kid on the block," computerized batteries are here to stay, but their utility will only be as good as the professionals who interpret the data that are collected by these procedures; i.e., computerized batteries are merely assessment devices that do not interpret the data.

The battery approach is not necessarily inconsistent with the flexible neuropsychological perspective advanced in this text and, in many instances, should complement the flexible battery approach by permitting the addition of key tasks and procedures that may not be available in single test measures or construct-specific batteries. Additionally, the advances asserted by the computerized assessment batteries permit rapid, efficient, and cost-effective assessment of mild brain injuries (e.g., concussions) that the traditional batteries do not necessarily permit. Their use in concussion management has set the bar for how concussion management should occur and likely has contributed to lessening second impact syndrome and the cumulative effects of multiple mild brain injuries in children and young adults. Consequently, the use of a neuropsychological battery in the assessment of children following a brain injury is not without merit and, with the appropriate training, this approach will continue to provide professionals with a variety of alternatives for neuropsychological assessment of children who have sustained a brain injury.

Chapter 13
Psychoeducational Assessment Procedures

Description

This will be the final chapter that discusses specific tests. For even the least experienced clinician or school professional, measures of psychoeducational assessment probably represent one of the least interesting aspects of this volume. Although these types of measures may not stimulate your palate for more, it is important to note that many of these tests are used routinely in neuropsychological assessment, particularly for children with brain injuries. For example, the Wechsler Adult Intelligence Scale and the Wechsler Intelligence Scale for Children, are among the most frequently used tests in neuropsychological assessments (Rabin et al., 2005). Further, when working with children, the clinical professional or educational diagnostician must have a working knowledge of school-related functions and academic skills assessment in particular. In that regard, it becomes important to mention key intellectual and academic achievement measures that undoubtedly will be given in whole or in part to a child or adolescent following a brain injury.

Findings in children and adolescents with brain injury

Many of the earlier research efforts examining the intellectual and academic outcomes of a brain injury utilized basic intelligence and achievement test batteries. Some of the initial studies in pediatric brain injury showed a decline in IQ from premorbid to post injury levels (Klonoff et al., 1977; Levin & Eisenberg, 1979a), with no more than a low average level of functioning being obtained following recovery for many children following a severe brain injury (Mayes et al,1989).

For children injured during the preschool years, there clearly appears to be a negative pattern associated with their intellectual functioning in the post acute phase as well as several years post injury. Ewing-Cobbs et al. (2006) found that 48% of their sample of children who sustained a TBI at approximately 21 months of age produced IQ scores that were below the 10th percentile, and longitudinal testing revealed persistent intellectual impairments with little in the way of recovery of intellectual functions. Taylor et al. (2008) found that their sample of children who were injured between three to six years of age obtained scores in the low average range of intelligence on the Differential Ability Scales about six weeks post injury, with findings being moderated by injury severity. A follow-up study by this group (Gerrard-Morris et al., 2009) revealed ongoing intellectual impairment at 6, 12, and 18 months post injury, particularly for the more severely injured group, with specific deficits in visual memory and executive functions being uncovered for the mild and moderate TBI groups. Anderson, Catroppa, Morse, Haritou, and Rosenfeld (2009) further demonstrated the pervasive intellectual impairment that can be seen following a severe brain injury in the preschool years five years post injury, with slower developmental trajectories being evident over this time span. Recovery curves for most cognitive abilities appeared to be the steepest during the 6 to 24 months post-injury (Ewing-Cobbs et al., 1997), with apparent stabilization by approximately 30 months post injury (Anderson et al., 2009).

For older children, findings from the Wechsler Intelligence Scale for Children have shown that nonverbal IQ seemed to be more affected than verbal IQ (Anderson et al., 2000; Arroyos-Jurado et al., 2006; Winogron et al., 1984), with little improvement being noted over an eight year time span for moderately to severely injured children (Arroyos-Jurado et al., 2006).

Approximately 30 years ago Boll (1983) noted that this pattern likely was due to the dependence of many of the subtests on the verbal scale being related to "old learning," whereas the nonverbal subtests were more dependent on efficiency, speeded accuracy, and novel problem solving. More recent efforts, however, how challenged the notion that the traditional "hold" measures of verbal ability are preserved as an indicator of premorbid cognitive abilities, or cognitive reserve (Satz, 1993; Fuentes, McKay, & Hay, 2010). Allen, Thaler, Donohue, and Mayfield (2010) used the WISC-IV with a sample of children with TBI and demonstrated the presence of deficits on all subtest and index scores, but particularly the Processing Speed Index. In contrast to earlier findings, however, these investigators did not show the expected disproportionate deficits in the Perceptual Reasoning Index.

To offset these contrary findings, other investigators (e.g., Thaler et al., 2010) have attempted to create subtypes of children with TBI using cluster analysis techniques. For example, using the subtests of the WISC-III, Thaler et al. (2010) demonstrated the presence of four reliable subtypes: Average, globally Impaired, Impaired Processing Speed, and Severe Perceptual Organization and Processing Speed. Initial validity of these cognitive clusters of children was demonstrated using parent behavior ratings wherein the globally impaired cluster was rated as having the most severe behavior problems. More generally, despite the debate on the pattern of intellectual abilities following a TBI, for many older children experiencing moderate to severe injuries it is unlikely that their intellectual functioning will return to pre-injury levels (Mayes et al., 1989) even at four (Filley et al., 1987) to five years post-injury (Klonoff et al., 1977), with ongoing deficits being reported 10 to 14 years after the insult (Horneman & Emanuelson, 2009; Jonsson, Horneman, & Emanuelson, 2004).

Interestingly, despite academic achievement being a core aspect of a child's day-to-day functioning, there have been precious few studies that have examined the academic functioning of children following a brain injury. Further, it would seem that the various neurocognitive impairments that children can manifest following a brain injury, such as slower speed of processing, disorganization, and planning problems, would lay the foundation for disrupted academic performance.

It is important to note the distinction here between an academic *skill deficit* versus a *performance deficit*. The former type of problem reflects an actual lack of knowledge pertaining to a specific academic domain or task (i.e., the skills have never been present or they have been encroached upon by the brain injury such that they are nonexistent). The performance deficit pertains to the poor execution of the skills necessary to demonstrate specific knowledge. This may occur when a child is unable to recall information efficiently, but perhaps recalls it at a later time. This distinction is critical in understanding how best to intervene with a specific child. For skill deficits, specific instruction in the academic area may be required, where as for performance deficits such teaching may be wasted energy, and they will require other approaches (e.g. retrieval strategies) to access the information.

Academic achievement problems can occur at any level of severity, including mild brain injuries (e.g., concussions) where significant inattention and disorganization may disrupt learning. Furthermore, given the disruption of higher-order language and discourse processes, the available literature shows that specific learning problems have been noted in all academic areas including reading (Catroppa et al., 2009; Ewing-Cobbs & Barnes, 2002; Ewing-Cobbs et al., 2006; Hanten et al., 2009; Hawley, Ward, Magnay, & Mychalkiw, 2004; Shaffer, Bijur, Chadwick, & Rutter, 1980), written language production and spelling (Catroppa et al., 2009; Ewing-Cobbs et al., 2006; Yorkston, Jaffe, Polissar, Liao, & Fay, 1997), and arithmetic (Catroppa et al., 2009; Ewing-Cobbs et al., 2006).

These problems persist and have been documented at two years post injury (Ewing-Cobbs, Fletcher, Levin, Iovino, & Miner, 1998), five years post-injury (Ewing-Cobbs et al., 2004), and nearly seven years post-injury (Catroppa et al., 2009). In addition, higher rates of special education and a failure to return to school historically have been reported. To illustrate this point, Michaud,

Rivara, Jaffe, Fay, and Dailey (1993), Donders (1994), and Ewing-Cobbs et al. (1998) reported rates that ranged between 50% to 79% of students requiring some form of special education following a brain injury. Further, Ewing-Cobbs et al. (2006) have provided evidence showing that nearly 50% of their sample of children with an early TBI (Mean age of injury = 21 months) had been retained in a grade and/or were receiving some form of special education. These rates were 18 times higher than for their non-injured peers. Arroyos-Jurado et al. (2006) also noted that parent report of higher premorbid achievement functioning was a significant predictor of later reading and spelling achievement skills six to eight years post injury—even more so than actual premorbid IQ. Taylor et al. (2008) arrived at similar conclusions for their sample of children who were injured during the preschool years wherein school readiness skills were compromised in the post acute period approximately 1-2 months post injury.

Finally, it is important to note that we have very little data on students who have sustained concussions and other milder forms of brain injury and their achievement skills. It is likely that many of these students also struggle significantly in the classroom setting as they move through recovery. Further, it is critical to make the observation of the time of year that the brain injury occurs as an injury that occurs later in the school year, or perhaps one that requires more time for the student to recover, actually may disrupt two school years. The academic consequences of this may be difficult to withstand without some form of educational support. This reinforces the notion that all of the state sports concussion laws should facilitate formal linkages back to the classroom setting so as to understand these "return-to-learn" situations in a more comprehensive and evidence-based fashion.

> **Finally, it is important to note that we have very little data on students who have sustained concussions and other milder forms of brain injury and their achievement skills. It is likely that many of these students also struggle significantly in the classroom setting as they move through recovery.**

Assessment Procedures

The psychoeducational assessment procedures actually represent the "bread and butter" for most school psychologists, educational diagnosticians, and other child practitioners. For most psychologists, the administration of various IQ and achievement tests is one of the first tasks that is addressed in graduate school. Over the past 20 years, though, many of our psychoeducational measures have changed to reflect more contemporary cognitive models and evidence-based findings with respect to the learning of reading, writing, and arithmetic.

Measures of intellectual functioning

Although the use of measures of intellectual functioning has come under fire, particularly with respect to their application to children with learning disabilities, they continue to have a purpose in the assessment of children following a brain injury. While I submit that the use of a full-blown IQ test may not be the best use of time in many clinical instances, the more contemporary models of intelligence offer greater multidimensionality in how neurocognitive processes are considered. Consequently, their utility in a more detailed description of a student's functioning is better realized and their potential to track change over time during recovery is greater.

There are a large number of intellectual batteries from which to choose, many of which are listed in Table 13.1. For the infant, toddler, and preschool age child, there is the Mullen Scales of Early Learning and the Bayley Scales of Infant Development-III. For the preschool child, school age child and adolescent, and adult, the age-appropriate Wechsler scale will provide a highly reliable and valid estimate of intellectual capabilities. In fact, each of these scales has been modified over the years to provide not just verbal and nonverbal measures of intelligence, but they have been retooled to provide additional indices addressing processing speed and working memory. The revised Wechsler Preschool and Primary Scale of Intelligence-4 also has added an Inhibitory Control measure that will extend findings into the executive functioning realm.

Similarly, the Stanford-Binet V and the Kaufman Assessment Battery for Children-II (KABC-II) provide contemporary avenues for intellectual appraisal that should facilitate not just a neuropsychological assessment approach via a flexible battery, but also should be useful for detailing the various neurocognitive strengths and weakness of an individual following a brain injury. Specifically, The Stanford-Binet V is based on the Cattell-Horn-Carroll model of intellectual functioning and is comprised of both verbal and nonverbal tasks that assess fluid reasoning, crystallized knowledge, quantitative reasoning, visual-spatial processing, and working memory. Consequently, there are a variety of findings that can be generated from this test that would support a profile analysis of a child's abilities following an injury. In addition, given that the test items were derived from contemporary test technology via Rasch-Wright Scaling, the Stanford-Binet V generates a Change Sensitive Score that can permit examination of change over time over serial assessments. Further, this test has a wide age range that extends from ages 2 to 90 years, and this should facilitate ongoing progress monitoring of various intellectual functions over the course of recovery and development.

Another intellectual measure that deserves mention is the KABC-II. The KABC-II is based on two modern theoretical models: the Cattell-Horn-Carroll Theory and Lurian Neuropsychological Theory. The examiner must decide which model to use in an a priori fashion, with a particular focus on whether a measure of crystallized intelligence is needed for the assessment. In this instance, the examiner would select the Cattell-Horn-Carroll theoretical model. For most children who have sustained a brain injury, this would be a critical addition to identifying spared versus impaired abilities secondary to the injury. The KABC-II comprises a total of 18 subtests that represent both core and supplementary procedures; however, if the Luria model is selected, then there are approximately five to eight core subtests at each age band, whereas if the Cattell-Horn-Carroll model is selected, then the assessment will require about seven to ten core subtests at each age band. Even the factor structure of the KABC-II is sophisticated in that the number of factors is age-dependent, thus capitalizing on the differences in neurocognitive abilities as a child ages. Specifically, age 3 has 1 factor (Fluid-Crystallized Index), the age band of 4 to 6 years has 4 factors (Sequential, Simultaneous, Learning, Knowledge), and the age band of 7 to 18 has 5 factors (Sequential, Simultaneous, Learning, Knowledge, Planning). Importantly, the KABC-II also provides a Nonverbal Scale and it has been co-normed with the Kaufman Test of Educational Achievement-II (KTEA-II).

> ... for children who are unable to talk following a brain injury, there are a variety of nonverbal assessments that should facilitate attainment of not only an overall level of intellectual function, but also an array of cognitive abilities.

Finally, for children who are unable to talk following a brain injury, there are a variety of nonverbal assessments that should facilitate attainment of not only an overall level of intellectual function, but also an array of cognitive abilities. For example, the Universal Nonverbal Intelligence Test (Bracken & McCallum, 2000) provide strategies for obtaining a multidimensional assessment of intellectual capabilities of a child who may be unable to speak or speak intelligibly, or perhaps who has a hearing impairment secondary to a brain injury. It was designed for children, ages 5 though 17 years wherein both administration and response are both nonverbal. The examiner uses eight universal hand and body gestures to explain the tasks to the child. Age-based standard scores are generated for reasoning, memory, symbolic, and nonsymbolic tasks, as well as for an overall Full Scale Intelligence Quotient. These Representative intellectual batteries can be seen in Table 13.1.

Table 13.1 Representative Measures of Intellectual Functioning.

Measures of Intellectual Functioning
Wechsler Intelligence Scale for Children-IV
Wechsler Adult Intelligence Scale-IV
Wechsler Preschool and Primary Scale of Intelligence-IV
Kaufman Assessment Battery for Children-II
Differential Abilities Scale-2
Stanford-Binet Intelligence Scale-V
Leiter International Performance Scale-3
Comprehensive Test of Nonverbal Intelligence-2
Universal Nonverbal Intelligence Test
Naglieri Nonverbal Abilities Test
Mullen Scales of Early Learning
Bayley Scales of Infant Development-III
Short-Forms of Intellectual Functioning
Kaufman Brief Intelligence Test-Revised
Wide Range Intelligence Test
Wechsler Abbreviated Scale of Intelligence-II
Reynolds Intellectual Assessment Scales
Stanford-Binet-V Abbreviated Scale of Intelligence
Woodcock-Johnson-III Brief Cognitive Scale

IQ Short-Forms

As can be seen in Table 13.1, there also is a growing number of short or abbreviated IQ tests that have become available in recent years. Most of us were taught not to consider intellectual short-forms for decision-making or dependable estimates of intellectual abilities as their reliability and validity were suspect. This is due, in large part, to the fact that these types of short forms were extracted versions from their parent measures (e.g., Sattler, 1988). Although some of the available short forms, such as the Stanford-Binet-V Abbreviated IQ and the Woodcock-Johnson III are derived from their longer parent batteries, many of the other short-forms represent stand-alone tests in their own right having their own normative base and psychometric properties. These tests represent a new genre in short-forms for intellectual assessment and, in fact, probably are not officially "short-forms" in that regard. For children with brain injuries, they also provide a more efficient strategy for obtaining an overall level of functioning, particularly in students with low stamina and poor attention regulation.

One example of this new genre of abbreviated measures of intelligence is the Wechsler Abbreviated Scale of Intelligence-II (WASI-II; Wechsler, 2012). The WASI-II was structured around the classic Wechsler scales as well as the fluid-crystallized model of cognitive abilities. In that regard, there are clearer linkages of the subtests to their child (WISC-IV) and adult (WAIS-IV) intelligence test counterparts, such that if a full intelligence scale is needed, the WASI-II subtests can be utilized to shorten the full battery and to preserve the derivation of the four factor scores from the larger scale. Further, the verbal subtests of Vocabulary and Similarities provide an estimate of Verbal Comprehension and associated crystallized abilities, whereas the nonverbal subtests of Block Design and Matrix Reasoning provide an estimate of Perceptual Reasoning and associated fluid abilities. Either a four-subtest or a two-subtest version can be employed depending on the amount of assessment time available or the stamina of the child.

A second example is the Reynolds Intelligence Assessment Scale (RIAS; Reynolds & Kamphaus, 2005). The RIAS is a superb example of how times have changed with respect to the consideration of "short-forms" in that the authors tout this test as "a reliable instrument that gives clinicians the information they need to make decisions about classification, selection, and educational placement." The RIAS was designed to be used with individuals from ages 3 through 94. It comprises two verbal, two nonverbal, and two supplementary memory tasks (one verbal and one nonverbal) which produce a Verbal Intelligence Index, a Nonverbal Intelligence Index, a Memory Index, and a Composite Intelligence Index. As such, this test provides a rapid and reliable assessment of both intellectual functioning and short-term memory across modalities, and it should serve examiners well in their assessment of students following a brain injury.

Academic achievement tests

The academic achievement tests are fairly straightforward in terms of their contribution to the assessment process. These tasks provide appraisals of selected academic functions, with some achievement batteries being more comprehensive in their coverage and other tests being more targeted in a specific academic domain. Following a brain injury, it will be important for the diagnostician to assess each of the academic domains for possible encroachment on academic functions as well as the child's ability to deploy knowledge across these domains (e.g., the presence of skill deficits versus performance deficits). A list of examples of both comprehensive and specific achievement tests is provided in Table 13.2.

Additionally, it is important to note that a comprehensive academic assessment will entail both formal achievement measures as well as informal measures. These latter assessment measures are critical in that they will depend on classroom observations, teacher reports, portfolio assessment, and a variety of curriculum based measures that will be directly tied to the child's day-to-day work. These assessment strategies also will facilitate the detection of whether there are true skill deficits which need to be remediated or whether there are performance deficits which will require other types of intervention beyond direct instruction of academic skills. Lastly, understanding the differences across these various academic assessment strategies should minimize the child's frustration with school and learning following the brain injury, and serve to facilitate ongoing positive academic progress.

Table 13.2 Representative Measures of Academic Achievement Skills.

Academic Achievement Tests-Comprehensive
Wide Range Achievement Test-4
Woodcock-Johnson Tests of Academic Achievement-III
Wechsler Individual Achievement Test-III
Peabody Individual Achievement Test-III
Kaufman-Test of Educational Achievement
Diagnostic Achievement Battery-3
Academic Achievement Tests-Specific
Woodcock Reading Mastery Test-3
Gray Oral Reading Test-5
Test of Word Reading Efficiency-2
Test of Reading Comprehension-4
Test of Early Reading Ability-3
Test of Early Written Language-3
Test of Written Language-4
Minnesota Handwriting Assessment
Test of Early Math Achievement-3
Key Math-3
Curriculum-Based Measures (CBM)

Summary

This chapter has dealt with the basic aspects of psychoeducational assessment as part of a larger evaluation of a child following a brain injury. There are a variety of intellectual and achievement measures to consider in the evaluation process, and these choices should be made carefully and deliberately in order to maximize the gains from the assessment, facilitate assessment-treatment linkages, and minimize the demands and frustrations to the child during the assessment proper. Further, many of the more contemporary measures of intelligence and achievement take into account current models of cognitive and academic functioning that are evidence-based, with many of the tests being far more multidimensional than their earlier predecessors. One relatively recent innovation pertains to the evolution of a new genre of abbreviated intelligence tests that stand alone with respect to their item development, psychometric properties, and normative data. These tools should have great promise for inclusion in the larger assessment of children following a brain injury. Lastly, while many of the comprehensive and specific achievement measures should provide good estimates of core academic skills, the infusion of informal measures, such as teacher observations, portfolio assessment, and curriculum based measures, should provide additional enrichment to understanding the nature of a child's academic struggles following a brain injury.

SECTION III
Related Assessment Issues

Chapter 14
Related Assessment Issues

Although a neuropsychological assessment perspective is recommended for evaluating children with a TBI (Silver et al., 2006), as illustrated in many of the preceding chapters the selection of an assessment approach and its associated measures for a particular child following a brain injury presents many choices and challenges. These choices and challenges are only a few facets of working with children following a brain injury and, indeed, there are a plethora of related assessment issues that can affect the evaluation process. The number of potential assessment-related issues here precludes the space allotments of this text, some of which actually may be unknown until presented by a specific clinical case, but several key issues are considered below.

Collection of Background Information

One major related assessment issue pertains to developing strategies to collect as much information as is feasible about the individual's pre-injury functioning level. This should be part of an evaluation process for any suspected disorder or disability; however, it becomes especially critical when evaluating a child or adolescent with a brain injury. In particular, obtaining a reliable developmental history, including prenatal, perinatal, and postnatal information, early well child visit findings, medical information, school functioning, and family history all become essential in terms of understanding a child's pre-injury functioning, the nature of the brain injury, and its effects on the child and the family system.

> One major related assessment issue pertains to developing strategies to collect as much information as is feasible about the individual's pre-injury functioning level. This should be part of an evaluation process for any suspected disorder or disability; however, it becomes especially critical when evaluating a child or adolescent with a brain injury.

While a thorough developmental and medical history is essential to understanding an individual's premorbid functioning, there have been a number of efforts to gain a more precise estimate of premorbid functioning (Lanham & Misukanis, 1999). These types of approaches include those that (1) use historical data that are indicative of past achievements; (2) examine post-injury test score levels; and (3) provide statistical combinations of targeted sociodemographic and psychometric information (Crawford, 1989; Vanderploeg, 1994). For example, such approaches have employed adult reading tests (Green et al., 2008), group administered achievement test scores extracted from school records (Baade & Schoenberg, 2004), and demographic information (Barona et al., 1984; Reynold & Gutkin, 1979).

More recent efforts have utilized the standardization sample from the WISC-IV to generate the Child Premorbid Intelligence Estimate (CPIE) to predict premorbid full scale IQ (Schoenberg, Lange, Brickell, & Saklofske, 2007).

The CPIE is comprised of 12 statistical algorithms to predict IQ, with one using solely demographic data and the other 11 employing various combinations of WISC-IV subtest raw scores with the demographic data. When applied to children with TBI, however, the CPIE was significantly different from a typically developing matched sample of children (Schoenberg et al., 2008), leading to cautions when using such estimating equations with a child following a brain injury. Further, Crawford (1989) and Veiel & Koopman (2001) have raised concerns about the lack of precision in these types of regression-based models in that they tend to overestimate the functioning in individuals with lower IQ and underestimate the functioning in individuals with higher IQ. In turn, this will affect how an examiner will interpret the degree of change in IQ following a TBI. Efforts have been proposed to address this bias in the regression-based models for estimating premorbid IQ (Veiel & Koopman, 2001), but these estimating equations should not supplant a good developmental history and related pre-assessment data collection procedures.

These pre-assessment data collection procedures require time and persistence, but may provide clues as to how a particular brain injury has affected the child in terms of learning, behavior, adaptive skills, social skills, and recreational activities. The effects of any post-injury problems, such as the development of a seizure disorder or persistent headaches, or the use of any medications, also will be critical to understand in terms of how they may influence the assessment results. Other medical findings, such as laboratory tests or various types of brain imaging scans (Brenner, Frier, Holshouser, Burley, & Ashwal, 2003; Babikian et al., 2006), may provide clues as to what to expect from the assessment. As part of obtaining the background information, it becomes critical to involve the family in this process because as noted in Chapter 11, these factors also can influence assessment findings as well as recovery trajectories.

Neurodevelopmental Constraints

The range of functioning for individuals with brain injuries is broad, and rates of recovery can vary from individual to individual. From an assessment perspective, challenges are presented by both higher and lower functioning individuals, as well as by children during the infancy, toddler, and preschool years versus the adolescent years (Ciccia, Meulenbroek, & Turkstra, 2009). It will be important for the examiner to take into account the issues of level of function and age of insult (Donders & Warschausky, 2007), particularly as these factors may influence the type of assessment approach and the specific assessment tasks that could be selected for an evaluation.

One major advantage of a construct-driven approach is that it provides the flexibility necessary to employ any test or measure, formal or informal, as well as data obtained from observations and interactions, into the assessment process. In other words, the challenges asserted by various neurodevelopmental constraints can readily be addressed by having this type of flexibility in the assessment process. In this regard, a thorough assessment of a child's functioning following a brain injury can occur at any developmental and/or severity level. Additionally, once a brain injury has occurred, especially one that is moderate to severe in nature, a developmental surveillance plan should be developed and instituted such that ongoing formal and/or informal assessments are conducted at planned time points in order to track individuals into at least the young adult transition phase of life (Horneman & Emanuelson, 2009; Jonsson et al., 2004).

> **These pre-assessment data collection procedures require time and persistence, but may provide clues as to how a particular brain injury has affected the child in terms of learning, behavior, adaptive skills, social skills, and recreational activities.**

Communication of Results

Communication of testing results is a critical component of the overall evaluation; i.e., how do you report the findings of your assessment? In general, most diagnosticians will have an interpretive meeting with the parents and child to discuss the results of the testing. Depending on the family situation, sometimes these meetings have everyone present and in other situations, they occur via different meetings with the parents versus the child. In most instances, findings also are communicated with physicians, therapists, and educational professionals via a written report. It is this written document that raises the most questions in terms of what it should contain and how to present the findings.

There are a variety of strategies that can be used to report the findings from the neurocognitive evaluation of a child who has sustained a brain injury. In many ways, these strategies are no different from those used for other medically-based conditions. In fact, some might argue that the only difference is embedded in specific features and characteristics that might exist from one condition to another. The flexible battery approach presented in this volume actually suggests a reasonably straightforward strategy for reporting results; that is, using the assessment constructs detailed in the earlier chapters. In this instance, once background information, the nature of the injury, and the presenting problems are detailed, each of the constructs can provide an organizing theme for presenting the specific findings. One major advantage to this strategy is that it requires diagnosticians to deal, up front, with inconsistencies in the test data. It also provides a vehicle for thinking about specific interventions that link to brain functions, rather than trying to extract interventions from tests or specific test scores. As an aside, while this text is not devoted to specific interventions, it should be a priority of the examiner to provide evidence-based recommendations when available, or best practices when possible; moreover, the examiner always should produce some data-based recommendations from their evaluation.

Team Evaluations and Approaches

Although a particular approach to assessment has been advanced in this text, the findings from this assessment approach should be inserted into an interdisciplinary team diagnostic conceptualization and associated intervention planning for that child and family. In fact, the Joint Committee on Interprofessional Relations between the American Speech-Language-Hearing Association and Division 40 (Clinical Neuropsychology) of the American Psychology Association (2007) have presented guidelines for how interdisciplinary teams should be organized and function for individuals with acquired brain injury. In part, these guidelines recommend that team members should include the individual, the family or caregiver network, a team coordinator knowledgeable in brain injury, and those professionals involved in the assessment and care of that individual following the injury.

The membership of the team can change depending on the severity of the injury, environmental demands, the nature and rate of the recovery process, or as new issues arise. It is important to note that an interdisciplinary team is different from a multidisciplinary team in that information is shared and integrated across providers, the individual, and the family/caregivers so as to arrive at a clear determination of diagnostic needs. In this fashion, the family has a voice in this process, and also will hear information in a less confusing and more coordinated format. Indeed, this type of approach will provide access to many different aspects of that child's functioning and recovery, and it will provide the family with a broad-based contact source from which to share information and express their concerns, particularly with respect to increasing their understanding of brain injury and the recovery process.

Further, in situations where the impact of a brain injury may have affected a particular set of functions, such as physical mobility or speech output, the input from a physical therapist or speech and language pathologist will be critical to that child and family within the broader context of recovery. Having access to a variety of different professionals who all understand brain injury—and who interact with one another—but who also have specific areas of expertise, should serve the individual better than a single professional, or even a loosely connected group of professionals. Relatedly, if a child is coming back to school from the hospital or rehabilitation setting, input on the current functioning status across a wide range of capabilities from these types of teams will provide invaluable information with respect to community and school transition needs and continuity of specific interventions.

Assessment-Treatment Linkages

While this text has placed its primary focus on assessment and assessment-related issues, we must not forget the definition of assessment that was proposed back in Chapter 1 (i.e., assessment as a problem solving process). In that regard, it becomes critical that the assessment findings serve to "solve a problem" that has been presented by the TBI.

One of those challenges comes in the form of what to do from an intervention perspective. Although a full discussion of the available best practices and evidence-based interventions is beyond the scope of this text, it is important that assessment data provide significant guidance with respect to serving children and their families following a TBI. Indeed, data are surfacing that support the use of neurocognitive findings to guide various interventions and to determine resource prioritization (O'Flaherty et al., 2000). Once impairments have been identified, evidence-based interventions to improve cognition, including the functions of attention (Galbiati et al., 2009), memory (Sjö, Spellerberg, Weidner, &Kihlgren, 2009), executive functions (Wade et al., 2010), and behavior (Feeney & Ylvisaker, 2003), should be instituted. A recent critical review of this literature reported encouraging findings pertaining to the effectiveness of these interventions (Ross, Dorris, & McMillan, 2011), but suggested the need for increased rigor in this area.

One final point on assessment-treatment linkages pertains to the increased use of computer-based applications for both assessment and intervention. The use of electronic devices for children and adolescents following a TBI to facilitate memory and organization has evidenced positive results (DePompei et al., 2008), and the list of Apps for brain injury rehabilitation is growing at an increasingly fast rate. For example, there are now Apps for assessment, communication, cognitive rehabilitation, and cognitive compensation (e.g., memory) (Sutton, 2012), and it is highly likely that the use of technology in the assessment-treatment process will only increase over time. Further, assessment may need to take into account what devices may be particularly important for a child as well as their capabilities and motivation to use the targeted device. Collaboration with an expert in assistive technology will be helpful here.

Community and School Re-Integration

From an assessment perspective, having a solid understanding of the premobid functioning and current functional status should serve to provide a strong foundation for returning a child to his or her community and school ecologies (Semrud-Clikeman, 2010). This is an issue that has been discussed for several decades (e.g., Ylvisaker, Hartwick, & Stevens, 1991), but to date there are few evidence-based models that exist to facilitate this transition process. At present, broad-based common sense (i.e.,

> The use of electronic devices for children and adolescents following a TBI to facilitate memory and organization has evidenced positive results (DePompei et al., 2008), and the list of Apps for brain injury rehabilitation is growing at an increasingly fast rate.

anecdotal) guidelines typically are employed (e.g., attends to a task for 10 to 15 minutes, can tolerate 20 to 30 minutes of classroom stimulation, can function adequately in a group of 2 or more students, engages in meaningful communication, follows simple directions accurately, gives some evidence of learning potential).

In general, if the transition is back to the school, it becomes important for the school interdisciplinary team to develop a plan to address these needs. This should include identification of the setting best suited for intervention (e.g., the formal school setting, homebound instruction, modified school day, etc.), re-evaluation at regular, predetermined time points, particularly in the case of acute injuries in order to accommodate changes over time, and awareness of special issues such as mobility and transportation needs (e.g., How will the child get to/from school? Once in school, how will they effectively move around the building?).

The school-based team should understand that there are very few commonalities among survivors. Individualization of programming likely will be critical to the successful re-integration of that child to the school setting. Finally, a strong neurodevelopmental surveillance plan should be developed in order to track progress and to evaluate the effectiveness of various intervention strategies. Sadly, for many children, school may be the only "rehabilitation facility" available; consequently, a careful determination of their needs is essential. Although a good neurodevelopmental surveillance plan should facilitate professionals in making appropriate adjustments to re-integration plans along the way, there are several promising models that provide strategies for facilitating the community and school re-integration process.

> **The school-based team should understand that there are very few commonalities among survivors. Individualization of programming likely will be critical to the successful re-integration of that child to the school setting.**

One model that exemplifies the notion of a mobile resource team is Brain STEPS (Strategies, Teaching, Educators, Parents, Students). The STEP Model is based on work examining the utility of the TBI Team Model (Glang et al., 2004) wherein both students and teachers seemed to benefit from training in TBI, technical assistance, and ongoing consultation pertaining to the services and interventions being provided to students. Further, these investigators noted that one of the most critical factors, in addition to injury severity, that will facilitate a child receiving formal special education services or other necessary educational supports is the quality of the communication between the hospital and the school (Glang et al., 2008). In this regard, the STEP program was instituted by the Brain Injury Association of Pennsylvania in 2007, in strong partnership with the state Department of Education's Bureau of Special Education (www.brainsteps.net). It involves the development of targeted brain injury consulting teams that are available to families and schools throughout the state of Pennsylvania. These teams are interdisciplinary in nature, with all of the members being trained in the educational needs of students returning to school following brain injury.

Teams work collaboratively with local school staff to develop educational programs, academic interventions, strategy implementation, and monitoring of students throughout the child's remaining academic years. One key facet of this program is that the teams are comprised of school, community, medical professionals, and families such that issues pertaining to communication across institutional boundaries can be addressed more readily. Team tasks span awareness, prevention, technical assistance around school re-entry, assessment, targeted interventions, and long-term monitoring. These teams also provide guidance to families with respect to available community resources, with a recent statewide model for concussion management by the schools being initiated.

Models such as Brain STEPS, and curriculum-based approaches (e.g., BrainSTARS; Dise-Lewis, Lewis, & Reichardt, 2009), provide linkages to interdisciplinary teams, emphasize the knowledge base of the professionals, and involve working with children and families from the time point of the injury through the recovery process—and beyond. The evidence-based aspects of these types of approaches remains to be determined at present, as do their sustainability, but they do represent best practices in models that link assessment findings to community and school re-integration. They also begin to confront the communication gaps that exist between major institutions (e.g., hospitals, schools, rehabilitation centers, community providers) serving children with TBI (Hawley et al., 2012), with more recent efforts extending into concussion management in the school setting (e.g., Sady, Vaughan, & Gioia, 2011).

Legal Ramifications

The legal issues that can arise following a brain injury should not be underestimated. It is not uncommon for "something" to happen to someone, and that "something" results in a brain injury. A fall on the playground during the school day during unsupervised play time, an injury that occurs during physical education or a sporting event, a motor vehicle accident, a gun shot wound, or a fist fight, to mention but a few instances where are brain injury can occur, all can be grounds for a legal case. Even though waivers are signed by parents, in many cases an astute attorney can find the loophole necessary to facilitate a legal proceeding. Quite frankly, if you work with children who have sustained a brain injury, it is highly likely that you will become involved in a legal proceeding at some point. Even in situations where an entity such as the school had nothing to do with the brain injury, children typically will be reintegrated back into the school setting at some point in the recovery process. School personnel will become involved simply because they are providing educational services to that child.

Outside of making the suggestion to obtain additional training in the legal issues surrounding a brain injury, and perhaps working closely with an attorney who knows this area well, professionals conducting assessments of children post-injury should take great care to stay within the confines of their assessment findings. Do not stray and make comments that do not align with your findings. For example, if you didn't assess a particular functional domain, note it. If you did assess a specific function, make sure you described what you saw and what you obtained. If you are not a neuropsychologist, then don't make brain-behavior associations….. you may be correct in your statements, but you will run the risk of being discredited by the opposing attorney given your lack of background and training in this area. This is law school 101!

Remember, the job of each attorney is to protect or advocate for their client, so everything will be fair game for scrutiny. This should not curtail your need to obtain a comprehensive assessment of a child or adolescent, but if you think about a legal possibility prior to your assessment, then you will be more fully prepared to address questions that may arise during the legal proceedings in the event that you are asked (or required!) to participate.

> **Quite frankly, if you work with children who have sustained a brain injury, it is highly likely that you will become involved in a legal proceeding at some point.**

Prevention

The primary focus of this text has been clearly focused on assessment-related issues, but the topic of brain injury is not completely addressed unless the issue of prevention is noted. The unfortunate fact is that most traumatic brain injuries could be avoided, or their severity lessened if a few preventative issues were addressed and/or if public policy required individuals to engage in preventative practices. For example, graduated driving licenses for adolescents clearly have contributed to dropping the number of motor vehicle accidents that this age group has experienced over the years. In turn, this has lessened the number of brain injuries secondary to this type of event in this age group.

For any parent with a teenager, there is a clear recognition of the significant differences between a young driver who is 18 versus 16 years old. Similarly, drunk driving laws, bicycle and motorcycle safety laws that require the use of helmets, improved sports equipment (e.g., football helmets), the increased use of return-to-play guidelines for both youth and professional sports, and the teaching of correct techniques to young athletes, particularly those involved in contact sports, all serve to increase awareness of safety pertaining to brain injuries as well as their prevention. In this regard, the Heads Up: Concussion in Youth Sports initiative, developed by the Center for Disease Control (www.cdc.gov/concussioninyouthsports), provides information about concussions to coaches, parents, and athletes involved in youth sports. This initiative includes information on preventing brain injuries in various sports (e.g., keeping the head up when making a tackle in football) as well as recognizing concussion symptoms and responding appropriately.

Although the evidence base for many of these practices and policies is continuing to evolve, there are some programs that clearly provide empirical support for prevention. One such program, the Period of PURPLE Crying (Barr et al., 2009) that can be see at the National Center on Shaken Baby Syndrome website (www.dontshake.org), pertains to the prevention of Abusive Head Trauma in infants and toddlers (i.e., Shaken Baby Syndrome). Inflicted brain injuries from Abusive Head Trauma have been documented to have a poor prognosis and high rates of neurocognitive and social-behavioral impairments (Barlow, Thomson, Johnson, & Minns, 2005); consequently, prevention of the abuse before it begins is paramount to reducing the incidence of this type of injury.

> **The sad fact is that most traumatic brain injuries could be avoided, or their severity lessened if a few preventative issues were addressed and/or if public policy required individuals to engage in preventative practices.**

The acronym PURPLE stands for:
- P – Peak of Crying (~2 to 16 weeks of age)
- U – Unexpected
- R – Resists Soothing
- P – Pain-Like Face
- L – Long Lasting (many hours)
- E – Evening

This program was designed to be conducted with new parents prior to leaving the hospital with their newborn infants. It comprises a simple straightforward approach to describing the basic fact that babies cry and parents get frustrated. In fact, the program capitalizes on developmental research showing that babies naturally will reach a peak of crying at approximately six weeks of age and that the amount of crying gradually declines over the next six weeks. It is no coincidence that this time period tends to be a major point of parent frustration and, in some instances, abuse resulting in a brain injury.

The Period of PURPLE Crying materials include a 10 minute DVD and an accompanying 11 page booklet, with parents generally being required to review these materials before they leave the hospital or at least before their first well child visit. The program is written at a third grade reading level, multicultural, and freely available in 10 different languages as well as for the hearing impaired. Several randomized control trials have found that the intervention group scored higher in their knowledge about crying and shaking, the dangers of shaking, and the strategy of walking away when they become frustrated with what feels like excessive crying. Additionally, there was a casual relationship found if the mothers read and watched the materials given to them, particularly with respect to increasing maternal knowledge and behaviors surrounding abusive head trauma.

As noted earlier in this volume, these types of early sustained injuries can have devastating effects on the neurodevelopmental status of that infant or toddler given that the brain is still in a rapid state of development at that time and the infant or toddler is defenseless. Hopefully, such programs contribute to preventing these types of injuries from occurring.

Knowledge, Knowledge, Knowledge

Just as in the real estate world where the mantra is location, location, location, for brain injury one of the mantras is knowledge, knowledge, knowledge. The terminology and phenomena that are associated with brain injuries are not well known to the general public; moreover, these issues are not overly familiar to many professionals. In fact, it has been shown that many of the myths about traumatic brain injury are endorsed by both lay people and professionals alike (Hooper et al., 2006). Educating survivors, families, professionals, and other consumers about the various nuances of brain injuries has been (Blosser & DePompei, 1991), and remains, an ongoing issue.

How does this affect the evaluation process? First and foremost, if someone does not recognize that a brain injury may have occurred, the discussion of possible interventions may never occur, with manifest behavior being attributed to other interpretations (e.g., volitional tendencies, psychiatric disorders, etc.). In these instances, it may be years later (or perhaps never) that a brain injury is linked to a learning and/or behavioral difficulty.

Second, even when a brain injury may have occurred, without knowledge of the potential seriousness of the injury and possible outcomes, a comprehensive assessment or management (e.g., in the case of a concussion) may never occur, or substandard care may be provided. In both of the first two points, this may place the individual at greater risk for a second brain injury and second impact syndrome, which can have life-long effects.

Third, without understanding the need for a thorough assessment following a brain injury, school services may not be pursued. In this regard, it becomes important for the evaluator to understand special education laws as well as available community resources, and to work toward suitable school accommodations to address learning and behavioral needs. Having good foundational knowledge in brain injury also will alert school and community professionals to the possibility that injuries sustained earlier in the child's development may not manifest their effects until challenged in later developmental time periods. Finally, by systematically training coaches, teachers, professionals, and other community providers in the nuances of brain injury, the need for a thorough assessment will be more easily facilitated.

In addition to the Brain STEPS Model described above, another systematic model that was designed to facilitate the development of assessment skills, primarily by school psychologists and related school professionals, has been instituted in the state of North Carolina (Hooper, 2003). This model has focused on providing professional development to school psychologists given their major role in the assessment, treatment, and ongoing monitoring of children and

> **Just as in the real estate world where the mantra is location, location, location, for brain injury one of the mantras is knowledge, knowledge, knowledge.**

adolescents who have sustained a brain injury; however, these professionals as well as other school-based providers typically have little specific training in brain injuries (Walker et al., 1999). In this regard, the North Carolina Training Model espoused a curriculum that addresses the core competencies of: (a) knowledge base for brain injury, (b) advanced assessment skills, and (c) intervention skills. Specific objectives and training mechanisms associated with each of these core competencies were designed as well.

This professional development program was developed to be comprehensive in nature and comprises two major components: didactic and clinical. The didactic component includes three different sessions that require approximately 36 hours of time. These sessions address basic information about brain injury, advanced assessment strategies and techniques, and specific (evidence-based when available) interventions. The clinical component requires the school psychologist to participate in 30 hours of case-based supervision with a neuropsychologist. To date, approximately 83% of school psychologists in the state have completed some or all of the training requirements, with about 30% completing all the requirements.

There have been ongoing challenges with all schools having access to a school psychologist trained in this model, but the model has been innovative in its development and noteworthy in its execution. Consequently, extending this type of knowledge across the state via the school psychology network has succeeded in at least increasing the awareness and knowledge base of professionals working in school and community settings. Hopefully, this has improved the school-based services to students following a brain injury.

Chapter 15
Epilogue

This book has been highly focused on key assessment approaches and strategies that should yield important findings in the evaluation of children and adolescents following a traumatic brain injury. An overview of the field of neuropsychology was provided as a backdrop for assessment of this population. The observations and findings that can be derived from such an assessment cannot be taken lightly given the complexity of various brain injuries, their dynamic nature, and the need to serve children and adolescents in an efficient and appropriate manner following such an event.

As detailed in the earlier chapters, several key neuropsychological assessment approaches were noted, each with their own array of strengths and weaknesses, but the one highlighted in this text was the flexible battery approach. This expanded assessment model provides for the use of targeted brain functions with the intent of viewing these functions in a multidimensional fashion. This multidimensionality allows for selective instruments selection, of course taking into account psychometric properties and neurodevelopmental constraints. It facilitates increased assessment-treatment linkages by keeping the data at the construct or subconstruct level.

Use of this approach, or one like it, will require the examiner to have a good understanding of brain functioning in children and adolescents, a working knowledge of brain injuries and their possible effects on various functions, and familiarity with a wide range of assessment tools and procedures. This text has provided representative options for examiners to consider when they engage in these types of assessment, but it is likely that the evaluators will have other options that are familiar to them and/or become available in the years ahead.

Finally, the array of issues inherent in doing a flexible assessment with children and adolescents following a brain injury is lengthy, with Chapter 14 only touching on a few of the many issues that could be addressed. Nonetheless, when working with this population, it will be prudent for the individual examiner(s) and team to be cognizant of the multiple potential issues that can appear with respect to a particular case. This will require a priori discussions, good up front data collection of background information and injury-related facts, and a carefully planned assessment.

Future Directions

As this text comes to a close, there are a few key issues that likely will drive future directions with respect to the assessment of pediatric brain injuries. First, this volume presented a construct-by-construct approach to thinking about the assessment of the child and adolescent following a brain injury. While this approach is likely one of the more common approaches used to perform such assessments, there has been a recent call to develop a common battery of measures to assess outcomes in pediatric brain injury. This proposal, developed by the Inter-Agency Pediatric Traumatic Brain Injury Outcomes Workgroup (McCauley et al., 2011), was asserted to facilitate a research agenda in the broad area of pediatric brain injury so as to encourage collaboration across sites and better comparison of research findings from study to study. Key recommendations from this workgroup included using specific measures to: (1) characterize the recovery process; (2) predict later outcomes; (3) reliably determine treatment effects; and, as noted above, (4) facilitate comparison of findings across studies. While the current text provided a cataloging, of sorts, of various assessment procedures available to clinicians, this workgroup recommended measures based on their proven utility with pediatric brain injury populations.

One clear advantage of having a common set of procedures is that it will facilitate the selection of constructs and associated measures for assessment. A second major advantage is that such an approach could advance our knowledge base with increased speed if studies were more comparable. In contrast, however, a one-size-fits alls approach will be a challenge given the complexity inherent across different types of brain injuries, the various mechanisms, injury severity, and the presence of various neurodevelopmental and environmental factors related to neurocognitive functioning and outcomes following a brain injury. The notion of a common set of assessment procedures is applauded, though, and future efforts likely will continue to explore these types of initiatives. The inclusion of computerized types of assessment, as well as utilization of computer devices in treatment, also should be considered.

A second major direction for the field will be to continue to pursue the special condition of concussion. The increased focus on concussion and mild brain injuries has called significant attention to the largest percentage of individuals who have sustained a brain injury. It has already begun to forge public policy discussions and changes across many aspects of our society. At a minimum, the discussions and media attention surrounding concussions sustained by our youth and professional athletes, as well as our military service members returning from war, have called significant attention to the awareness of brain injury. The awareness efforts have contributed to increasing the knowledge base of lay individuals and professionals alike in the area of brain injuries. From an assessment perspective, though, we are only beginning to gain an understanding of how to assess individuals who have sustained a concussion, and the impact of concussion on the neurological development of children and adolescents is only beginning to be understood. Future directions likely will continue to refine our assessment approaches, make them more available to community and school settings, and increase evidence-based efforts with respect to not only return-to-play but also return-to-learn management and practices. One last comment on this point, concussion serves as a great reminder that not all children will require special education services; however, all children with a concussion should be considered for some type of educational modification in order to facilitate their recovery AND to support their ongoing learning needs in the school setting.

A final major direction, and one that has been ongoing, is the continued push for different levels of intervention. For example, at the awareness and prevention levels in brain injury, a number of formal training programs have emerged, many from state brain injury associations, and it is hoped that their extension to a wider variety of professionals will continue to be pursued. Similarly, while continuing education opportunities in TBI will persist, the topic of brain injury typically is not covered in the degree-granting programs of our colleges, universities, and other institutes of higher learning. This should be advanced. For example, just as it is highly likely that a regular classroom teacher will have a child with a reading problem in their class, it also is reasonable to assume that a child with a brain injury will be in that class as well. In this regard, it will be important for programs that prepare teachers and other childhood professionals—including physicians—to expand their content to include information related to pediatric brain injuries and how they can affect a child's day-to-day functioning across many different aspects of their life. Needless to say, the push for more rigorous research to advance evidence-based intervention programs remains critical to the secondary and tertiary intervention levels, and should guide the assessment-treatment process.

The advances in pediatric brain injury over the past 10 to 20 years have been impressive, but it is likely that the advances over the next 10 to 20 years will be even more fruitful. Undoubtedly, our knowledge of what happens to the brains of children and adolescents following a brain injury will morph in exciting ways. The application of that knowledge should facilitate new and better approaches to assessment and treatment. Further, with the rapid changes in technology, the assessment and intervention strategies that are available to professionals working with this population will increase as well. While these innovations will fuel the field, it remains for clinicians and interdisciplinary teams to continue to work towards improved systems-of-care for children with brain injuries and their families, such as the proposed Pediatric Acquired Brain Injury network (https://www.thebrainproject.org). Such national networks have the potential to cross agency boundaries and connect within and across specific communities/regions in order to promote a more orderly system-of-care for children and their families following a TBI. Needless to say, a comprehensive assessment of a child's functioning following a brain injury will remain a core component of these future directions, and such systems will promote more rapid care and increased access to necessary resources for all children.

> **The advances in pediatric brain injury over the past 10 to 20 years have been impressive, but it is likely that the advances over the next 10 to 20 years will be even more fruitful.**

References

Achenbach, T. M. (2009). The Achenbach System of Empirically Based Assessment (ASEBA): Development, findings, theory, and applications. Burlington, VT: University of Vermont Research Center for Children, Youth and Families.

Achenbach, T.M., & Edelbrock, C. (1983). Manual for the Child Behavior Checklist and Revised Child Behavior Profile. Burlington, VT: University Associates in Psychiatry.

Allen, D.N., Leany, B.D., Thaler, N.S., Cross, C., Sutton, G.P., & Mayfield, J. (2010). Memory and attention profiles in pediatric traumatic brain injury. Archives of Clinical Neuropsychology, 25, 618-633.

Allen, D.N., Thaler, N.S., Donohye, B., & Mayfield, J. (2010). WISC-IV profiles in children with traumatic brain injury: Similarities to and differences from the WISC-III. Psychological Assessment, 22, 57-64.

American Academy of Pediatrics Subcommittee on Attention-Deficit/Hyperactivity Disorder Steering Committee on Quality Improvement and Management (2011). ADHD: Clinical Practice Guideline for the Diagnosis, Evaluation, and Treatment of Attention-Deficit/Hyperactivity Disorder in Children and Adolescents. Pediatrics, 128, 1-16.

American Psychiatric Association, (2013). Diagnostic and Statistical Manual of Mental Disorders (Fifth Edition). Washington, DC: Author.

Anderson, V.A., Anderson, P., Northam, E., Jacobs, R., & Catroppa, C. (2001). Development of executive functions through late childhood and adolescence in an Australian sample. Developmental Neuropsychology, 20, 385-406.

Anderson, V., Brown, S., & Newitt, H. (2010). What contributes to quality of life in adult survivors of childhood traumatic brain injury? Journal of Neurotrauma, 27, 863-870.

Anderson, V., Brown, S., Newitt, H., & Hoile, H. (2009). Educational, vocational, psychosocial, and quality-of-life outcomes for adult survivors of childhood traumatic brain injury. Journal of Head Trauma Rehabilitation, 24, 303-312.

Anderson, V., Brown, S., Newitt, H., & Hollie, H. (2011). Long-term outcome from childhood traumatic brain injury: Intellectual ability, personality, and quality of life. Neuropsychology, 25, 176-184.

Anderson, V., & Catroppa, C. (2007). Memory outcome at 5 years post-childhood traumatic brain injury. Brain Injury, 21, 1399-1409.

Anderson, V.A., Catroppa, C., Haritou, F., Morse, S., & Rosenfeld, J.V. (2005). Identifying factors contributing to child and family outcome 30 months after traumatic brain injury in children. Journal of Neural Neurosurgeon Psychiatry, 76, 401-408.

Anderson, V.A., Catroppa, C., Morse, S.A., & Haritou, F. (1999). Functional memory skills following traumatic brain injury in young children. Developmental Neurorehabilitation, 3, 159-166.

Anderson, V., Catroppa, C., Morse, S., Haritou, F., & Rosenfeld, J. V. (2009). Intellectual outcome from preschool traumatic brain injury: A 5-year prospective, longitudinal study. Pediatrics, 124, 1064-1072.

Arroyos-Jurado, E., Paulsen, J.S., Ehly, S., & Max, J.E. (2006). Traumatic brain injury in children and adolescents: Academic and intellecutal outcomes following injury. Exceptionality: A Special Education Journal, 14, 125-140.

Arroyos-Jurado, E., Paulsen, J.S., Merrell, K.W., Lindgren, S.D., & Max, J.E. (2000). Traumatic brain injury in school-age children: Academic and social outcomes. Journal of School Psychology, 38, 571-587.

Atchison, B.T., Fisher, A.G., & Bryze, K. (1998). Rater reliability and internal scale and person response validity of the School Assessment of Motor and Process Skills. American Journal of Occupational Therapy, 52, 843-850.

Baade, L.E., & Schoenberg, M.R. (2004). A proposed method to estimate premorbid intelligence utilizing group achievement measures from school records. Archives of Clinical Neuropsychology, 19, 227-243.

Babikian, T., & Asarnow, R. (2009). Neurocognitive outcomes and recovery after pediatric TBI: Meta-analytic review of the literature. Neuropsychology, 23, 283-296.

Babikian, T., Freier, M.C., Ashwal, S., Riggs, M.L., Burley, T., & Holshouser, B.A. (2006). MR spectroscopy: Predicting long-term neuropsychological outcome following pediatric TBI. Journal of Magnetic Resonance Imaging, 24, 801-811.

Babikian, T., Satz, P., Zaucha, K., Light, R., Lewis, R.S., & Asarnow, R.F. (2011). The UCLA Longitudinal Study of Neurocognitive Outcomes Following Mild Pediatric Traumatic Brain Injury. Journal of the International Neuropsychological Society, 17, 886-895.

Barca, L., Cappelli, F.R., Amicuzi, L., Apicella, M.G., Castelli, E., & Stortini, M. (2009). Modality-specific naming impairment after traumatic brain injury. Brain Injury, 23, 920-929.

Barkley, R.A. (1997). ADHD and the nature of self-control. New York: Guilford.

Barkley, R.A. (2001). The executive functions and self-regulation: An evolutionary neuropsychological perspective. Neuropsychology Review, 11, 1-29.

Barkovich, A.J., & Raybaud, C. (2012). Pediatric neuroimaging. Philadelphia: Lippincott, Williams, & Wilkins.

Barlow, K.M., Thomas, E., Johnson, D., & Minns, R.A. (2005). Late neurologic and cognitive sequelae of inflictured traumatic brain injury in infancy. Pediatrics, 116, 174-186.

Barona, A., Reynolds, C.R., & Chastain, R. (1984). A demographically based index of pre-morbid intelligence for the WAIS-R. Journal of Consulting and Clinical Psychology, 52, 885-887.

Barr, R., Rivara, F., Barr, M. (2009). Effectiveness of educational materials designed to change knowledge and behaviors regarding crying and shaken-baby syndrome of newborns: A randomized, controlled Trial. Pediatrics, 123, 972-980.

Bawden, H.N., Knights, R.M., & Winogron, H.W. (1985). Speeded performance following head injury in children. Journal of Clinical and Experimental Neuropsychology, 7, 39-54.

Bedell, G.M., & Dumas, H.M. (2004). Social participation of children and youth with acquired brain injuries discharged from inpatient rehabilitation: a follow-up study. Brain Injury, 18, 65-82.

Beers, S.R., Wisniewski, S.R., Garcia-Filioin, P., Tian, Y., Hahner, T., Berger, R.P., et al. (2011). Validity of a pediatric verson of the Glasgow Outcome Scale-Extended. Journal of Neurotrauma, 29, 1126-1139.

Berling, K., Knutsson, J., Rosenblad, A., & von Unge, M. (2011). Evaluation of electrogustometry and the filter paper disc method for taste assessment. Acta Otolaryngology, 131, 488-493.

Bloom, D.R., Levin, H.S., Ewing-Cobbs, L., Saunders, A.E., Song, J., Fletcher, J.M., et al. (2001). Lifetime and novel psychiatric disorders after pediatric traumatic brain injury. Journal of the American Academy of Child and Adolescent Psychiatry,

Blosser, R., & DePompei, J. (1991). Preparing education professionals for meeting the needs of students with traumatic brain injury. Journal of Head Trauma Rehabilitation, 6, 73-82.

Boll, T.J. (1983). Minor head injury in children-Out of sight but not out of mind. Journal of Clinical Child Psychology, 12, 74-80.

Bornhofen, C., & McDonald, S. (2008). Emotion perception deficits following traumatic brain injury: A review of the evidence and rationale for intervention. Journal of the International Neuropsychological Society, 14, 511-515.

Bracken, B., & McCallum, S. (2000). Universal Nonverbal Intelligence Test. Rolling Meadows, IL: Riverside Publishing.

Brenner, T., Freier, M.C., Holshouser, B.A., Burley, T., & Ashwal, S. (2003). Predicting neuropsychologic outcome after traumatic brain injury in children. Pediatric Neurology, 28, 104-114.

Brooks, D.N. (1983). Disorders of memory. In M. Rosenthal, E.R. Griffith, M.R. Bond, & J.D. Miller (Eds.), Rehabilitation of the head injured adult (pp. 185-196). Philadelphia: F.A. Davis.

Brown, G., Chadwick, O., Shaffer, D., Rutter, M., & Traub, M. (1981). A prospective study of children with head injuries: III. Psychiatric sequelae. Psychological Medicine, 11, 63-78.

Bruce, A. E., Cole, D. A., Dallaire, D. H., Jacques, F. M., Pineda, A. Q., & LaGrange, B. (2006). Relations of parenting and negative life events to cognitive diathesis for depression in children. Journal of Abnormal Child Psychology, 34, 321-333.

Bruce, D.A., & Zimmerman, R.A. (1989). Shaken impact syndrome. Pediatric Annals, 18, 492-494.

Bryden, M.P. (1982). Laterality: Functional asymmetry in the intact brain. New York: Academic Press.

Cantor, J.B., Gordon, W.A., Schwartz, M.E., Charatz, H.J., Ashman, T.A., & Abramowitz, S. (2004). Child and parent responses to a brain injury screening questionnaire. Archives of Physical Medicine and Rehabilitation, 85 (4, Suppl 2), S54-S60.

Carlson, C.I. (2003). Assessing the family context. In C.R. Reynolds, & R.W. Kamphaus (Eds.), Handbook of psychological and educational assessment of children: Personality, behavior, and context (3rd ed.) (p. 473-492). New York: The Guilford Press.

Carlson, S.M., Moses, L.J., & Claxton, L.J. (2004). Individual differences in executive functioning and theory of mind: An investigation of inhibitory control and planning ability. Journal of Experimental Child Psychology, 87, 299-319.

Catroppa, C., & Anderson, V. (2005). A prospective study of the recovery of attention from acute to 2 years following pediatric traumatic brain injury. Journal of the International Neuropsychological Society, 11, 84-98.

Catroppa, C., & Anderson, V. (2009). Neurodevelopmental outcomes of pediatric traumatic brain injury. Future Neurology, 4, 811-821.

Catroppa, C., & Anderson, V. (2006). Planning, problem-solving and organizational abilities in children following traumatic brain injury: Intervention techniques. Developmental Neurorehabilitation, 9, 89-97.

Catroppa, C., & Anderson, V.A. (2003). Recovery and predictors of intellectual ability two years following paediatric traumatic brain injury. Neuropsychological Rehabilitation: An International Journal, 13, 517-536.

Catroppa, C., & Anderson, V. (2004). Recovery and predictors of language skills two years following pediatric traumatic brain injury. Brain and Language, 88, 68-78.

Catroppa, C., & Anderson, V. (2007). Recovery in memory function, and its relationship to academic success, at 24 months following pediatric TBI. Child Neuropsychology, 13, 240-261.

Catroppa, C., Anderson, V.A., Morse, S.A., Haritou, F., & Rosenfeld, J.V. (2007). Children's attentional skills 5 years post-TBI. Jounal of Pediatric Psychology, 32, 354-369.

Catroppa, C., Anderson, V.A., Morse, S.A., Haritou, F., & Rosenfeld, J.V. (2008). Outcome and predictors of functional recovery 5 years following pediatric traumatic brain injury (TBI). Journal of Pediatric Psychology, 33, 707-718.

Catroppa, C., Anderson, V.A., Muscara, F., Morse, S.A., Haritou, F., Rosenfeld, J.V., et al. (2009). Educational skills: Long-term outcome and predictors following paediatric traumatic brain injury. Neuropsychological Rehabilitation: An International Journal, 19, 716-732.

Chadwick, O., Rutter, M., Brown, G., Shaffer, D., & Traub, M. (1981). A prospective study of children with head injuries: II. Cognitive sequelae. Psychological Medicine, 11, 49-61.

Chadwick, O., Rutter, M., Shaffer, D., & Shrout, P.E. (1981). A prospective study of children with head injuries: IV. Specific cognitive deficits. Journal of Clinical Neuropsychology, 3, 101-120.

Chaplin, D., Deitz, J., & Jaffe, K.M. (1993). Motor performance in children after traumatic brain injury. Archives of Physical Medicine and Rehabilitation, 74, 161-164.

Chapman, S.B., Gamino, J.F., Cook, L.G., Hanten, G., Li, X., & Levin, H.S. (2006). Impaired discourse gist and working memory in children after brain injury. Brain and Language, 97, 178-188.

Chapman, S.B., Sparks, G., Levin, H.S., Dennis, M., Roncadin, C., Zhang, L., et al. (2004). Discourse macrolevel processing after severe pediatric traumatic brain injury. Developmental Neuropsychology, 25, 37-60.

Chevignard, M.P., Catroppa, C., Galvin, J., & Anderson, V. (2010). Development and evaluation of an ecological task to assess executive functioning post childhood TBI: The Children's Cooking Task. Brain Impairment, 11, 125-143.

Ciccia, A.H., Meulenbroek, P., & Turkstra, L.S. (2009). Adolescent brain and cognitive development: Implication for clinical assessment in traumatic brain injury. Topics in Language Disorders, 29, 249-265.

Colvin, J.D., Thurm, C., Pate, B.M., Newland, J.G., Hall, M., & Meehan, W.P. (April, 2012). Incidence and management of concussions at children's hospitals. Paper presented at The Pediatric Academic Societies Annual Meeting, Boston, Massachusetts.

Conklin, H.M., Salorio, C.F., & Slomine, B.S. (2008). Working memory performace following paediatric traumatic brain injury. Brain Injury, 22, 847-857.

Corrigan, J.D., & Bogner, J. (2007). Initial reliability and validity of the Ohio State University TBI identification method. Journal of Head Trauma Rehabilitation, 22, 318-329.

Crawford, J.R. (1989). Estimation of premorbid intelligence: A review of recent developments. In J.R. Crawford, & D.M. Parker (Eds.), Developments in clinical and experimental neuropsychology (pp. 55-74). New York: Plenum.

Daigneault, S., Braün, C.M.J., & Whitaker, H.A. (1992). An empirical test of two opposing theoretical models of prefrontal function. Brain and Cognition, 19, 48-71.

Davidson, R.J. (1993). Cerebral asymmetry and emotion: Conceptual and methodological conundrums. Cognition and Emotion, 7, 115-138.

Delis, D.C. (2012). Delis-Rating of Executive Functions (D-REF). San Antonio, TX: Pearson.

Dellatolas, G., Filho, G.B., Braga, L.W., & Souza, L.M. (2007). Quality-of-life: Child and parent perspectives following severe traumatic brain injury. Developmental Neurorehabilitation, 10, 35-47.

Delis, D.C., Kaplan, E., & Kramer, J.H. (2001). Delis-Kaplan Executive Function System (D-KEFS). San Antonio, TX: Pearson.

Denckla, M.B. (1996). A theory and model of executive function. In G.R. Lyon, & N.A. Krasnegor (Eds.), Attention, memory, and executive function (pp. 263-278). Baltimore: Paul H. Brookes Publishing Company.

Denenberg, V.H. (1983). Lateralization of function in rats. American Journal of Physiology, 245, R505-R509.

Dennis, M. (1991). Frontal lobe function in childhood and adolescence: A heuristic for assessing attention regulation, executive control, and the intentional states important for social discourse. Developmental Neuropsychology. 7, 327-358.

Dennis, M., Agostino, A., Roncadin, C., & Levin, H. (2009). Theory of mind depends on domain-general executive functions of working memory and cognitive inhibition in children with traumatic brain injury. Journal of Clinical and Experimental Neuropsychology, 31, 835-847.

Dennis, M., Purvis, K.L., Barnes, M.A., Wilkinson, M., & Winner, E. (2001). Understanding of literal truth, ironic criticism, and deceptive praise following childhood head injury. Brain and Language, 78, 1-16.

Dennis, M., Simic, N., Taylor, H.G., Bigler, E.D., Rubin, K., Vannatta, K., Gerhardt, C.A., Stancin, T., Roncadin, C., & Yeates, K.O. (2012). Theory of mind in children with traumatic brain injury. Journal of the International Neuropsychological Society, 18, 908-916.

DePompei, R., Gillette, Y., Goetz, E., Xenopoulos-Oddsson, A., Bryen, D., & Dowds, M. (2008). Practical application for use of PDAs and smartphones with children and adolescents who have traumatic brain injury. NeuroRehabilitation, 23, 487-499.

Dettmer, J.L., Daunhauer, L., Detmar-Hanna, D., & Smple, P.L. (2007). Putting brain injury on the radar: exploratory reliability and validity analyses of the Screening Tool for Identification of Acquired Brain Injury in school-aged children. Journal of Head Trauma Rehabilitation, 22, 339-349.

Dimitrijevic, M.M., Dimitrijevic, M.R., Kinalski, R., McKay, W.B., & Sherwood, A.M. (1987). Neurophysiological assessment of motor disorders in patients with brain injury. In M.E. Minor, & K.A. Wagner (Eds.), Neurotrauma: Treatment, rehabilitation and related issues No. 2 (pp. 81-88). Boston: Butterworths.

Dise-Lewis, J.E., Lewis, H.C., & Reichardt, C.S. (2009). BrainSTARS: Pilot data on a team-based intervention program for students who have acquired brain injury. Journal of Head Trauma Rehabilitation, 24, 166-177.

Donders, J. (1993). Memory functioning after traumatic brain injury in children. Brain Injury, 7, 431-437.

Donders, J. (1994). Academic placement after traumatic brain injury. Journal of School Psychology, 32, 53-55.

Donders, J., & Hoffman, N.M. (2002). Gender differences in learning and memory after pediatric traumatic brain injury. Neuropsychology, 16, 491-499.

Donders, J., & Warschausky, S. (2007). Neurobehavioral outcomes after early versus late childhood traumatic brain injury. Journal of Head Trauma Rehabilitation, 22, 296-302.

Dumas, M.H., & Carey, T. (2002). Motor skill and mobility recovery outcomes of children and youth with traumatic brain injury. Physical & Occupational Therapy in Pediatrics, 22, 73-99.

Emslie, H., Wilson, C., Burden, V., Nimmo-Smith, I., & Wilson, B. (2003). Behavioural Assessment of Dysexecutive Syndrome for Children (BADS-C). Titchfield, Hants: Thames Valley Tests Company.

Epstein, N.B. & Bishop, D.S. (1993). The McMaster Assessment Device (FAD). In F. Walsh (Ed.), Normal Family Processes. New York: Guilford Press.

Erickson, S.J., Montague, E.Q., Gerstle, M.A. (2010). Health-related quality of life in children with moderate-to-severe traumatic brain injury. Developmental Neurorehabilitation, 13, 175-181.

Espy, K.A., Kaufmann, P.M., McDiarmid, M.D., & Glisky, M.L. (1999). Executive functioning in preschool children: Performance on A-Not-B and other delayed response format tasks. Brain and Cognition, 41, 178-199.

Ewing-Cobbs, L., & Barnes, M. (2002). Linguistic outcomes following traumatic brain injury in children. Seminars in Pediatric Neurology, 9, 209-217.

Ewing-Cobbs, L., Barnes, M., Fletcher, J.M., Levin, H.S., Swank, P.R., & Song, J. (2004). Modeling of longitudinal academic achievement scores after pediatric traumatic brain injury. Developmental Neuropsychology, 25, 107-133.

Ewing-Cobbs, L., Brookshire, B., Scott, M.A., & Fletcher, J.M. (1998). Children's narratives following traumatic brain injury: Lingusitic structure, cohesion, and thematic recall. Brain and Language, 61, 395-419.

Ewing-Cobbs, L., & Fletcher, J.M. (1987). Neuropsychological assessment of head injury in children. Journal of Learning Disabilities, 20, 526-535.

Ewing-Cobbs, L., Fletcher, J.M., & Levin, H.S. (1986). Neurobehavioral sequelae following head injury in children: Educational implications. Journal of Head Trauma Rehabilitation, 1, 57-65.

Ewing-Cobbs, L., Fletcher, J.M., Levin, H.S., Francis, D.J., Davidson, K., & Miner, M.E. (1997). Longitudinal neuropsychological outcome in infants and preschoolers with traumatic brain injury. Journal of the International Neuropsychological Society, 3, 581-591.

Ewing-Cobbs, L., Fletcher, J.M., Levin, H.S., Iovino, I., & Miner, M.E. (1998). Academic achievement and academic placement following traumatic brain injury in children and adolescents: A two-year longitudinal study. Journal of Clinical and Experimental Neuropsychology, 20, 769-781.

Ewing-Cobbs, L., Fletcher, J.M., Levin, H.S., & Landry, S.H. (1985). Language disorders after pediatric head injury. In J.K. Darby (Ed.), Speech and language evaluation in neurology: Childhood disorders (pp. 97-112). Orlando, FL: Grune & Stratton.

Ewing-Cobbs, L., Levin, H.S., Eisenberg, H.M., & Fletcher, J.M. (1987). Language functions following closed head injury in children and adolescents. Journal of Clinical and Experimental Neuropsychology, 9, 575-592.

Ewing-Cobbs, L., Levin, H.S., Fletcher, J.M., Miner, M.E., & Eisenberg, H.M. (1990). The Children's Orientation and Amnesia Test: Relationship to severity of acute head injury and to recovery of memory. Neurosurgery, 27, 683-691.

Ewing-Cobbs, L., Prasad, M., Fletcher, J.M., Levin, H.S., Miner, M.E., & Eisenbery, H.M. (1998). Attention after pediatric traumatic brain injury: A multidimensional assessment. Child Neuropsychology, 4, 35-48.

Ewing-Cobbs, L., Prasad, M.R., Kramer, L., Cox, C.S., Baumgartner, J., Fletcher, J.M., et al. (2006). Late intellectual and academic outcomes following traumatic brain injury sustrained during early childhood. Journal of Neurosurgery, 105, 287-296.

Ewing-Cobbs, L., Prasad, M.R., Landry, S.H., Kramer, L., & DeLeon, R. (2004). Executive function following traumatic brain injury in young children: A preliminary analysis. Developmental Neuropsychology, 26, 487-512.

Ewing-Cobbs, L., Prasad, M.R., Swank, P., Kramer, L., Cox Jr., C.S., Fletcher, J.M., et al. (2008). Arrested development and disrupted callosal microstructure following pediatric traumatic brain injury: relation to neurobehavioral outcomes. NeuroImage, 42, 1305-1315.

Feeney, T.J., & Ylvisaker, M. (2003). Context-sensitive behavioral supports for young children with TBI: Short-term effects and long-term outcome. Journal of Head Trauma Rehabilitation, 18, 33-51.

Fennell, E.B., & Mickle, J.P. (1992). Behavioral effects of head trauma in children and adolescents. In M.G. Tramontana & S.R. Hooper (Eds.), Advances in child neuropsychology (Vol. I, pp. 24-49). New York: Springer-Verlag.

Filley, C.M., Cranberg, L.D., Alexander, M.P., & Hart, E.J. (1987). Neurobehavioral outcome after closed head injury in childhood and adolescence. Archives of Neurology. 44, 194-198.

Fletcher, J.M., Ewing-Cobbs, L., Miner, M.E., Levin, H.S., & Eisenberg, H.M. (1990). Behavioral changes after closed head injury in children. Journal of Consulting and Clinical Psychology, 58, 93-98.

Fletcher, J.M., Miner, M.E., & Ewing-Cobbs, L. (1987). Age and recovery from head injury in children: Developmental issues. In H.S. Levin, J. Grafman, & H.M. Eisenberg (Eds.), Neurobehavioral recovery from head injury (pp. 279-291). New York: Oxford University Press.

Fletcher, J.M., & Taylor, H.G. (1984). Neuropsychological approaches to children: Towards a developmental neuropsychology. Journal of Clinical Neuropsychology, 6, 39-56.

Flor-Henry, P. (1979). On certain aspects of the localization of the cerebral systems regulating and determining emotion. Biological Psychiatry, 14, 677-698.

Fuld, P.A., & Fisher, P. (1977). Recovery of intellectual ability after closed head injury. Developmental Medicine and Child Neurology, 19, 495-502.

Fuentes, A.M., & Hay, C. (2010). Cognitive reserve in paediatric traumatic brain injury: Relationship with neuropsychological outcome. Brain Injury, 24, 995-1002.

Gagnon, I., Forget, R., Sullivan, S.J., & Friedman, D. (1998). Motor performances following a mild traumatic brain injury in children: an exploratory study. Brain Injury, 12, 843-853.

Galbiati, S., Recia, M., Pastore, V., Liscio, M., Bardoni, A., Castello, E., et al. (2009). Attention remediation following traumatic brain injury in childhood and adolescence. Neuropsychology, 23, 40-49.

Gale, S.D., & Prigatano, G.P. (2010). Deep white matter volume loss and social reintegration after traumatic brain injury in children. Journal of Head Trauma Rehabilitation, 25, 15-22.

Galvin, J., Elspeth, F.H., & Imms, C. (2009). Sensory processing abilities of children who have sustained traumatic brain injuries. The American Journal of Occupational Therapy, 63, 701-709.

Ganesalingam, K., Sanson, A., Anderson, V., & Yeates, K.O. (2007). Self-regulation as a mediator of the effects of childhood traumatic brain injury on social and behavioral functioning. Journal of the International Neuropsychological Society, 12, 298-311.

Geary, E.K., Kraus, M.F., Pliskin, N.H., & Litle, D.M. (2010). Verbal learning differences in chronic mild traumatic brain injury. Journal of the International Neuropsychological Society, 16, 506-516.

Gerrard-Morris, A., Taylor, H.G., Yeates, K.O., Walz, N.C., Stancin, T., & Minich, N. (2010). Cognitive development after traumatic brain injury in young children. Journal of the International Neuropsychological Society, 16, 157-168.

Gioia, G.A., Isquith, P.K., Guy, S.C., & Kenworthy, L. (2000). Behavior Rating Inventory of Executive Function. Odessa, FL: Psychological Assessment Resources.

Gioia, G.A., & Isquith, P.K. (2004). Ecological assessment of executive function in traumatic brain injury. Developmental Neuropsychology, 25, 135-158.

Giza, C.C., & Havda, D.A. (2001). The neurometabolic cascade of concussion. Journal of Athletic Training, 36, 228-235.

Glang, A., Todis, B., Thomas, C.W., Hood, D., Bedell, G., & Cockrell, J. (2008). Return to school following childhood TBI: Who gets services? NeuroRehabilitation, 23, 477-486.

Glang, A., Tyler, J., Pearson, S., Todis, B., & Morcant, M. (2004). Improving educational services for students with TBI through statewide consulting teams. NeuroRehabilitation, 19, 219-231.

Goldman-Rakic, P.S., & Friedman, H.R. (1991). The circuitry of working memory revealed by anatomy and metabolic imaging. In Levin, H.S., Eisenberg, H.M., & Benton, A.L. (Eds.), Frontal lobe function and dysfunction (pp. 72-91). New York: Oxford University Press.

Grattan, L.M., & Eslinger, P.J. (1991). Frontal lobe damage in adults and children: A comparative review. Developmental Neuropsychology, 7, 283-326.

Greene, R.E., Melo, B., Christensen, B., Ngo, L.A., Monette, G., & Bradbury, C. (2008). Measuring premorbid IQ in traumatic brain injury: an examination of the validity of the Wechsler Test of Adult Reading (WTAR). Journal of Clinical and Experimental Neuropsychology, 30, 163-172.

Gualtieri, C.T., & Johnson, L.G. (2006). Reliability and validity of a computerized neurocognitive test battery, CNS Vital Signs. Archives of Clinical Neuropsychology, 21, 623–643.

Gulbrandsen, G.B. (1984). Neuropsychological sequela of light head injuries in older children six months after trauma. Journal of Clinical Neuropsychology, 6, 257-268.

Gustavson, J.L., Golden, C.J., Wilkening, G.N., Hermann, B.P., Plaisted, J.R., Macdnnes, W.D., & Leark, R.A. (2004). The Luria-Nebraska Neuropsychological Battery-Children's Revision: Validation with brain-damaged and normal children. Journal of Psychoeducational Assessment, 2, 199-208.

Haarbauer-Krupa, J. (2012). Schools as TBI service providers. The ASHA Leader, July 3, 10-21.

Hahn, Y.S., Chyung, C., Barthel, M.J., Bailes, J., Flannery, A., & MeLone, D.G. (1988). Head injuries in children under 36 months of age. Child's Nervous System, 4, 34-40.

Hamilton, N.A., & Keller, M.S. (2010). Mild traumatic brain injury in children. Seminars in Pediatric Surgery, 19, 271-278.

Hanten, G., Bartha, M., & Levin, H.S. (2000). Metacognition following pediatric traumatic brain injury: A preliminary study. Developmental Neuropsychology, 18, 383-398.

Hanten, G., Dennis, M., Zhang, L., Barnes, M., Roberson, G., Archibald, J., et al. (2004). Childhood head injury and metacognitive processes in language and memory. Developmental Neurology, 25, 85-106.

Hanten, G., Li, X., Newsome, M.R., Swank, P., Chapman, S.B., Dennis, M., et al. (2009). Oral reading and expressive language after childhood traumatic brain injury: Trajectory and correlates of change over time. Topics in Language Disorders, 29, 236-248.

Hanten, G., Wilde, E.A., Menefee, D.S., Li, X., Lane, S., Vasquez, C., et al. (2008). Correlates of social problem solving during the first year after traumatic brain injury in children. Neuropsychology, 22, 357-370.

Hanten, G., Zhang, L., & Levin, H.S. (2002). Selective learning in children after traumatic brain injury: A preliminary study. Child Neuropsychology, 8, 107-120.

Hawley, C.A., Ward, A.B., Mahanay, A.R., & Mychalkiw, W. (2004). Return to school after brain injury. Archives of Diseases of Childhood, 89, 136-142.

Heffelfinger, A.K., & Koop, J.I. (2009). A description of preschool neuropsychological assessment in the P.I.N.T. Clinic after the first 5 years. The Clinical Neuropsychologist, 23, 51-76.

Heiden, J., Small, R., Canton, W., Weiss, M., & Kurtze, T. (1983). Severe head injury. Journal of the American Physical Therapy Association, 63, 4-9.

Heugten, C.M., Hendriksen, J., Rasquin, S., Dijcks, B., Jaeken, D., & Vles, J.H. (2006). Long-term neuropsychological performance in a cohort of children and adolescents after severe paediatric traumatic brain injury. Brain Injury, 20, 895-903.

Hongwanishkul, D., Happaney, K.R., Lee, W.S.C., & Zelazo, P.D. (2005). Assessment of hot and cool executive function in young children: Age-related changes and individual differences. Developmental Neuropsychology, 28, 617-644.

Hooper, S.R., Alexander, J., Moore, D., Sasser, H.C., Laurent, S., King, J., Bartel, S., & Callahan, B. (2004). Caregiver reports of common symptoms in children following a traumatic brain injury. NeuroRehabilitation, 19, 175-189.

Horneman, G., & Emanuelson, I. (2009). Cognitive outcome in children and young adults who sustained severe and moderate traumatic brain injury 10 years earlier. Brain Injury, 23, 907-914.

Horneman, G., Folkesson, P., Sintonen, H., von Wendt, L., & Emanuelson, I. (2005). Health-related quality of life of adolescents and young adults 10 years after serious traumatic brain injury. International Journal of Rehabilitation Research, 28, 245-249.

Horton, A.M., Soper, H.V., & Reynolds, C.R. (2010). Executive functions in children with traumatic brain injury. Applied Neuropsychology: Adult, 17, 99-103.

Hughes, C. (1998). Executive function in preschoolers: Links with theory of mind and verbal ability. British Journal of Developmental Psychology, 16, 233–253.

Iselin, G., Brocque, R.L., Kenardy, J., Anderson, V., & Mcinlay, L. (2010). Which method of posttraumatic stress disorder classification best predicts psychosocial function in children with traumatic brain injury? Journal of Anxiety Disorders, 24, 774-779.

Jaffe, K.M., Polisar, N.L., Fay, G.C., & Liao, S. (1995). Recovery trends over three years following pediatric traumatic brain injury. Archives of Physical Medicine and Rehabilitation, 76, 17-26.

Janusz, J.A., Kirkwood, M.W., Yeates, K.O., & Taylor, H.G. (2002). Social problem-solving skills in children with traumatic brain injury: Long-term outcomes and prediction of social competence. Child Neuropsychology, 8, 179-194.

Jefferson, A.L., Paul, R.H., Ozonoff, A., & Cohen, R.A. (2006). Evaluating elements of executive functioning as predictors of instrumental activities of daily living (IADLs). Archives of Clinical Neuropsychology, 21, 311-320.

Jennett, B. (1986). Head trauma. In A.K. Asbury, G.M. McKhann, & W.I. McDonald (Eds.), Diseases of the nervous system (pp. 1282-1291). Philadelphia: W.B. Saunders.

Joint Committee on Interprofessional Relations Between the American Speech-Language-Hearing Association and Division 40 (Clinical Neuropsychology) of the American Psychological Association (2007). Structure and function of an interdisciplinary team for persons with acquired brain injury [Guidelines]. Available from www.asha.org/policy.

Johnson, A.R., Dematt, E., & Salorio, C.F. (2009). Predictors of outcome following acquired brain injury in children. Developmental Disabilities Research Reviews, 15, 124-132.

Jonsson, C.A., Horneman, G., & Emanuelson, I. (2004). Neuropsychological progress during 14 years after severe traumatic brain injury in childhood and adolescence. Brain Injury, 18, 921-934.

Jordan, F.M., Ozanne, A.E., & Murdoch, B.E. (1990). Performance of closed head injured children on a naming task. Brain Injury, 4, 27-32.

Jorge, R.E. (2005). Neuropsychiatric consequences of traumatic brain injury: a review of recent findings. Current Opinion in Psychiatry, 18, 289-299.

Josman, N., Berney, T., & Jarus, T. (2000). Performance of children with and without traumatic brain injury on the Contextual Memory Test (CMT). Physical & Occupational Therapy in Pediatrics, 19, 39-51.

Kapapa, T., Pfister, U., Konig, K., Sasse, M., Woischneck, D., Heissler, H.E., et al. (2010). Head trauma in children, part 3: Clinical and psychosocial outcomes after head trauma in children. Journal of Child Neurology, 25, 409-422.

Karver, C.L., Wade, S.L., Cassedy, A., Taylor, H.G., Stancin, T., Yeates, K.O., & Walz, N.C. (2012). Age at injury and long-term behavior problems after traumatic brain injury in young children. Rehabilitation Psychology, 57, 256-265.

Kirkwood, M., Janusz, J., Yeates, K.O., Taylor, H.G., Wade, S.L., Stancin, T., et al. (2000). Prevalence and correlates of depressive symptoms following traumatic brain injuries in children. Child Neuropsychology, 6, 195-208.

Klonoff, H., Low, M.D., & Clark, D. (1977). Head injuries in children: A prospective five year follow-up. Journal of Neurology, Neurosurgery, and Psychiatry, 40, 1211-1219.

Klonoff, H., & Paris, R. (1974). Immediate, short-term and residual effects of acute head injuries in children: Neuropsychological and neurological correlates. In R.M. Reitan, & L.A. Davison (Eds.), Clinical neuropsychology: Current status and applications (pp. 179-219). New York: John Wiley.

Korkman, M., Kemp, S.L., & Kirk, U. (2001). Effects of age on neurocognitive measures of children ages 5 to 12: A cross-sectional study on 800 children from the United States. Developmental Neuropsychology, 20, 331-354.

Kramer, M.E., Chiu, P., Shear, P.K., & Wade, S.L. (2009). Neural correlates of verbal associative memory and mnemonic strategy use following childhood traumatic brain injury. Journal of Pediatric Rehabilitation Medicine, 2, 255-271.

Krawczyk, D.C., Hanten, G., Wilde, E.A., Li, X., Schnelle, K.P., Merkley, T.L., et al. (2010). Deficits in analogical reasoning in adolescents with traumatic brain injury. Frontiers in Human Neuroscience, 4, 1-13.

Krasnegor, N.A., Lyon, G.R., Goldman-Rakic, P.S. (Eds.) (1996). Development of prefrontal cortex (pp. 265-281). Baltimore: Paul H. Brookes Publishing Company.

Kuhtz-Buschbeck, P.J., Hoppe, B., Golge, M., Dreesmann, M., Damnn-Stunitz, U., & Ritz, A. (2003). Sensorimotor recovery in children after traumatic brain injury: analyses of gait, gross motor, and fine motor skills. Developmental Medicine & Child Neurology, 45, 821-828.

Lajiness-O'Neill, R., Erdodi, L., & Bigler, E.D. (2010). Memory and learning in pediatric traumatic brain injury: A review and examination of moderators of outcome. Applied Neuropsychology: Adult, 17, 83-92.

Langlos, J.A., Rutland-Brown, W., & Wald, M.M. (2006). The epidemiology and impact of traumatic brain injury. Journal of Head Trauma Rehabilitation, 21, 375-378.

Lanham, R.A., & Misurkanis, T. (1999). Estimating premorbid intelligence. Determining change in cognition following a brain injury. Brain Injury Source, 3, 1-5.

Leblanc, N., Chen, S., Swank, P.R., Ewing-Cobbs, L., Barnes, M., Dennis, M., et al. (2005). Response inhibition after traumatic brain injury (TBI) in children: Impairment and recovery. Developmental Neuropsychology, 28, 829-848.

Lehnung, M., Leplow, B., Herzog, A., Benz, B., Ritz, A., Stolze, H., et al. (2001). Children's spatal behavior is differentially affected after traumatic brain injury. Child Neuropsychology, 7, 59-71.

Lehnung, M., Leplow, B., Ekroll, V., Benz, B., Ritz, A., Mehdorn, M., et al. (2003). Recovery of spatial memory and persistence of spatial orientation deficits after traumatic brain injury during childhood. Brain Injury, 17, 855-869.

Lehmkuhl, G., & Thoma, W. (1990). Development in children after severe head injury. In. A. Rothenberger (eds.), Brain and behavior in child psychiatry (pp. 267-282). Berlin: Springer-Verlag.

Letswaart, M., Crawford, J.R., & Currie, D. (2008). Social behavior following traumatic brain injury and its association with emotional recognition, understanding of intentions, and cognitive flexibility. Journal of the International Neuropsychological Society, 14, 318–326.

Levin, H.S., Benton, A.L., & Grossman, R.G. (Eds.) (1982). Neurobehavioral consequences of closed head injury. New York: Oxford University Press.

Levin, H.S., & Eisenberg, H.M. (1979a). Neuropsychological impairment after closed head injury in children and adolescents. Journal of Pediatric Psychology, 4, 389-402.

Levin, H.S., & Eisenberg, H.M. (1979b). Neuropsychological outcome of closed head injury in children and adolescents. Child's Brain, 5, 281-292.

Levin, H.S., Hanten, G., Roberson, G., Li, X., Ewing-Cobbs, L., Dennis, M., et al. (2008). Prediction of cognitive sequelae based on abnormal computel tomography findings in children following mild traumatic brain injury. Journal of Neurosurgery Pediatrics, 1, 461-470.

Levin, H.S., & Hanten, G. (2005). Executive functions after traumatic brain injury in children. Pediatric Neurology, 33, 79-93.

Levin, H.S., Hanten, G., Zhang, L., Swank, P.R., Ewing-Cobbs, L., Dennis, M., et al. (2004). Changes in working memory after traumatic brain injury in children. Neuropsychology, 18, 240-247.

Levin, H.S., Hanten, G., Zhang, L., Swank, P.R., & Hunter, J. (2004). Selective Impairment of inhibition after TBI in children. Journal of Clinical and Experimental Neuropsychology, 26, 589-597.

Levin, H.S., High, W.M., Ewing-Cobbs, L., Fletcher, J.M., Eisenberg, H.M., Miner, M.E., & Goldstein, F.C. (1988). Memory functioning during the first year after closed head injury in children and adolescents. Neurosurgery, 22, 1043-1052.

Levin, H.S., O'Donnell, V.M., & Grossman, R.G. (1979). The Galveston Orientation and Amnesia Test: A practical scale to assess cognition after head injury. Journal of Nervous and Mental Disease, 167, 675-684.

Levin, H.S., Song, J., Ewing-Cobbs, L., & Roberson, G. (2001). Porteus Maze performance following traumatic brain injury in children. Neuropsychology, 15, 557-567.

Lezak, M.D., Howieson, D.B., & Loring, D.W. (2004). Neuropsychological assessment (4th ed.). New York: Oxford University Press.

Lieh-Lai, M.W., Theodorou, A.A., Samaik, A.P., Meert, K.L., Moylan, P.M., & Canady, A.I. (1992). Limitations of the Glasgow Coma Scale in predicting outcome in children with traumatic brain injury. Journal of Pediatrics, 120, 195-199.

Limond, J., Dorris, D., & McMillan, T.M. (2009). Quality of life in children with acquired brain injury: Parent perspectives 1–5 years after injury. Brain Injury, 23, 617-622.

Lovell, M.R., Iverson, G.L., Collins, M.W., Podell, K., Johnston, K.M., Pardini, D., et al. (2006). Measurement of symptoms following sports-related concussion: Reliability and normative data for the post-concussion scale. Applied Neuropsychology, 13, 166–174.

Lowther, J.L., & Mayfield, J. (2004). Memory functioning in children with traumatic brain injuries: a TOMAL validity study. Archives of Clinical Neuropsychology, 19, 105-118.

Luis, C.A., & Mittenberg, W. (2002). Mood and anxiety disorders following pediatric traumatic brain injury: A prospective study. Journal of Clinical and Exerimental Neuropsychology, 24, 270-279.

Luria, A.R. (1966). Human brain and psychological process. New York: Harper & Row.

MacNeill, A., Soper, H.V., & Reynolds, C.R. (2010). Executive functions in children with traumatic brain injury. Applied Neuropsychology: Adult, 17, 99-103.

Madigan, N.K., DeLuca, J., Diamond, B.J., Tramontano, G., & Averill, A. (2000). Speed of information processing in traumatic brain injury: Modality-specific factors. Journal of Head Trauma Rehabilitation, 15, 943-956.

Madsen, S.N., Spellerberg, S., Weidner, S., & Kihlgren, M. (2009). Training of attention and memory deficits in children with acquired brain injury. ACTA Paediatrica, 99, 230-236.

Maillard-Wermelinger, A., Yeates, K.O., Taylor, H.G., Rusin, J., Bangert, B., Dietrich, A., et al. (2009). Mild traumatic brain injury and executive functions in school-aged children. Developmental Neurorehabilitation, 12, 330-341.

Mandalis, A., Kinsella, G., Ong, B., & Anderson, V. (2007). Working memory and new learning following pediatric traumatic brain injury. Developmental Neuropsychology, 32, 683-701.

Mangeot, S., Armstrong, K., Colvin, A.N., Yeates, K.O., & Taylor, H.G. (2002). Long-term executive function deficits in children with traumatic brain injuries: Assessment using the Behavior Rating Inventory of Executive Function (BRIEF). Child Neuropsychology, 8, 271-284.

Manly, T., Robertson, I.H., Anderson, V., & Nimmo-Smith, I. (1998). The Test of Everyday Attention for Children (TEA-Ch). San Antonio, TX: Pearson.

Max, J.E., Castillo, C.S., Lindgren, S.D., & Arndt, S. (1998). The Neuropsychiatric Rating Schedule: reliability and validity. Journal of the American Academy of Child and Adolescent Psychiatry, 37, 297-304.

Max, J.E., Koele, S.L., Lindgren, S.D., Robin, D.A., Smith, W.L., Sato, Y. (1998). Adaptive functioning following traumatic brain injury and orthopedic injury: A controlled study. Archives of Physical Medicine and Rehabilitation, 79, 893-899.

Max, J.E., Loele, S.L., Castillo, C.C., Lindgren, S.D., Arndt, S., Bokura, H., (2000). Personality change problem in children and adolescents following traumatic brain injury. Journal of the International Neuropsychological Society, 6, 279-289.

Max, J.E., Robin, D.A., Lindgren, S.D., Smith, W.L., Sato, Y., Mattheis, P.J., et al. (1997). Traumatic brain injury in children and adolescents: Psychiatric disorders at two years. Journal of the American Academy of Child and Adolescent Psychiatry, 36, 1276-1285.

Mayes, S.D., Pelco, L.E., & Campbell, C.J. (1989). Relationships among pre- and post injury intelligence, length of coma, and age in individuals with severe closed head injuries. Brain Injury, 3, 301-313.

Mazzocco, M.M.M., & Kover, S.T. (2007). A longitudinal assessment of executive function skills and their association with math performance. Child Neuropsychology, 13, 18-45.

McCarthy, M.L., MacKenzie, E.J., Durbin, D.R., Aiken, M.E., Jaffe, K.M., Paidas, C.N., et al. (2006). Health-related auality of life during the first year after traumatic brain injury. Archives of Pediatric and Adolescent Medicine, 160, 252-260.

McCauley, S.R., & Levin, H.S. (2004). Prospective memory in pediatric traumatic brain injury: A preliminary study. Developmental Neuropsychology, 25, 5-20.

McCauley, S.R., Pedroza, C., Chapman, S.B., Cook, L.G., Hotz, G., Vasquez, A.C., et al. (2010). Event-based prospective memory performance during subacute recovery following moderate to severe traumatic brain injury in children: Effects of monetary incentives. Journal of the International Neuropsychological Society, 16, 335-341.

McCauley, S.R., Wilde, E.A., Anderson, V.A., Bedell, G., Beers, S.R., Campbell, T.F., et al. (2012). Recommendation for the use of common outcome measures in pediatric traumatic brain injury research. Journal of Neurotrauma, 29, 678-705.

McCauley, S.R., Wilde, E.A., Merkley, T.L., Schnelle, K.P., Bigler, E.D., Hunter, J.V., et al. (2010). Patterns of cortical thinning in relation to event-based prospective memory performance three months after moderate to severe traumatic brain injury in children. Developmental Neuropsycholgy, 35, 318-332.

McConaughy, S. H., & Achenbach, T. M. (2001). Manual for the Semistructured Clinical Interview for Children and Adolescents (2nd ed.). Burlington, VT: University of Vermont, Center for Children, Youth, & Families.

McCrea, M., Guskiewicz, K., Randolph, C., Barr, W.B., Hammeke, T.A., Marshall, S.W., Powell, M.R., Woo Ahn, K., Wang, Y., & Kelly, J.P. (2012). Incidence, clinical course, and predictors of prolonged recovery time following sport-related concussion in high school and college athletes. Journal of the International Neuropsychological Society, 18, 1-12.

McKinlay, A. (2009). Controversies and outcomes associated with mild traumatic brain injury in childhood and adolescenes. Child care, health and development, 36, 3-21.

McKissock, W., Richardson, A., & Bloom, W.H., (1960). Subdural hematoma. A review of 389 cases. Lancet, 228, 1365-1369.

Menkes, J.H., Sarat, H.B., & Maria, B.L. (2005). Child neurology (7th ed.). Lippincott, Williams, & Wilkins.

Michaud, L.J., Rivara, F.P., Jaffe, K.M., Fay, G., & Dailey, J.L. (1993). Traumatic brain injury as a risk factor for behavioral disorders in children. Archives of Physical Medicine and Rehabilitation, 74, 368-375.

Milberg, W.P.Hebben, N.A., & Kaplan, E. (2009). The Boston process approach to neuropsychological assessment. In I. Grant, & K. Adams. Neuropsychological assessment of neuropsychiatric disorders (3rd ed.). New York: Oxford University Press.

Milders, M., Fuchs, S., & Crawford, J.R. (2003). Neuropsychological impairments and changes in emotional and social behaviour following severe traumatic brain injury. Journal of Clinical and Experimental Neuropsychology, 25, 157-172.

Miller, L.J., & Donders, J. (2003). Prediction of educational outcome after pediatric traumatic brain injury. Rehabilitation Psychology, 48, 237-241.

Miller, L.J., & Lane, S.J. (2000). Toward a consensus in terminology in sensory integration theory and practice. Part I: Taxonomy of neurophysiological processes. Sensory Integration: Special Interest Section Quarterly, 23, 1-4.

Mirsky, A.F., Anthony, B.F., Duncan, C.C., Ahearn, M.B., & Kellam, S.G. (1991). Analysis of the elements of attention: A neuropsychological approach. Neuropsychological Review, 2, 109-145.

Miyake, A., Friedman, N.P., Emerson, M.J., Witzki, A.H., & Howerter, A. (2000). The unity and diversity of executive functions and their contributions to complex "frontal lobe" tasks: A latent variables analysis. Cognitive Psychology, 41, 49-100.

Moore, D.W., Ashman, T.A., Cantor, J.B., Krinick, R.J., & Spielman, L.A. (2010). Does gender influence cognitive outcome after traumatic brain injury? Neuropsychological Rehabilitation: An International Journal, 20, 340-354.

Moran, C.A., Nippold, M.A., & Gallion, G.T. (2006). Working memory and proverb comprehension in adolescents with traumatic brain injury: A preliminary investigation. Brain Injury, 20, 417-423.

Morgan, A., Ward, E., & Murdoch, B. (2004). Clinical progression and outcome of dysphagia following paediatric traumatic brain injury: a prospective study. Brain Injury, 18, 359–376.

Morse, S., Haritou, F., Ong, K., Anderson, V., Catroppa, C., & Rosenfeld, J. (1999). Early effects of traumatic brain injury on young children's language performance: a preliminary linguistic analysis. Developmental Neurorehabilitation, 3, 139-148.

Mottram, L., & Donders, J. (2006). Cluster subtypes on the California Verbal Learning Test- Children's Version after pediatric traumatic brain injury. Developmental Neuropsychology, 30, 865-883.

Muscara, F., Catroppa, C., & Anderson, V. (2008). Social problem-solving skills as a mediator between executive function and long-term social outcome following paediatric traumatic brain injury. The British Psychological Society, 2, 445-461.

Muscara, F.M., Catroppa, C., & Anderson, V. (2008). The impact of injury severity on executive function 7-10 years following pediatric traumatic brain injury. Developmental Neuropsychology, 33, 623-636.

Nadebaum, C., Anderson, V., & Catroppa, C. (2007). Executive function outcomes following traumatic brain injury in young children: A five year follow-up. Developmental Neuropsychology, 32, 703-728.

Naglieri, J.A., & Goldstein, S. (2013). Comprehensive Executive Function Inventory (CEFI). North Tonawanda, NY: MHS, Inc.

Nance, M.L., Polk-Williams, A., Collins, M.W., & Wiebe, D.J. (2009). Neurocognitive evaluation of mild traumatic brain injury in the hospitalized pediatric population. Annals of Surgery, 249, 859-863.

National Head Injury Foundation (1985). An educator's manual: What educators need to know about students with traumatic brain injury. Framingham, MA: Author.

Newsome, M.R., Steinberg, J.L., Scheibel, R.S., Troyanskaya, M., Chu, Z., Hanten, G., et al. (2008). Effects of traumatic brain injury on working memory-related brain activation in adolescents. Neuropsychology, 22, 419-425.

Nolin, P. (2006). Executive memory dysfunctions following mild traumatic brain injury. Journal of Head Trauma Rehabilitation, 21, 68-75.

O'Flaherty, S.J., Chivers, A., Hannan, T. J., Kendrick, L.M., McCartney, L.C., Wallen, M.A., et al. (2000). The Westmead Pediatric TBI Multidisciplinary Outcome Study: Use of functional outcomes data to determine resource prioritization. Archives of Physical Medicine Rehabilitation, 81, 723-729.

Olson, D. (2011). FACES-IV and the circumplex model: Validation study. Journal of Marital & Family Therapy, 3, 64-80.

Park, B.S., Allen, D.N., Barney, S.J., Ringdahl, E.N., & Mayfield, J. (2009). Structure of attention in children with traumatic brain injury. Applied Neuropsychology: Adult, 16, 1-10.

Pennington, B. (1997). Dimensions of executive functions in normal and abnormal development. In N. A. Krasnegor, G. R. Lyon, & P. S. Goldman-Rakic (Eds.), Development of prefrontal cortex (pp. 265-281). Baltimore: Paul H. Brookes Publishing Company.

Pentland, L., Todd, J.A., & Anderson, V. (1998). The impact of head injury severity on planning ability in adolescence: A functional analysis. Neuropsychology Rehabilitation: An International Journal, 8, 301-317.

Petersen, C., Scherwath, A., Fink, J., & Koch, U. (2008). Health-related quality of life and psychosocial consequences after mild traumatic brain injury in children and adolescents. Brain Injury, 22, 215-221.

Posner, M., & Petersen, S.E. (1990). The attention system of the human brain. Annual Review of Neuroscience, 13, 25-42.

Prigatano, G.P., & Gray, J. (2008). Parental perspectives on recovery and social reintegration after pediatric traumatic brain injury. Journal of Head Trauma Rehabilitation, 23, 378-387.

Prigatano, G.P., Gray, J.A., & Gale, S.D. (2008). Individual case analysis of processing speed difficulties in children with and without traumatic brain injury. The Clinical Neuropsychologist, 22, 603-619.

Prigatano, G.P., & Gupta, S. (2006). Friends after traumatic brain injury in children. Journal of Head Truma Rehabilitation, 21, 505-513.

Reynolds, C.R., & Gutkin, T.B. (1979). Predicting the premorbid intellectual status of children using demographic data. Clinical Neuropsychology, 1, 36-38.

Reynolds, C.R., & Kamphaus, R.W. (2005). Reynolds Intelligence Assessment Scales. Odessa, FL.: PAR

Riggs, N.R., Jahromi, L.B., Razza, R.P., Dilworth-Bart, J.E., & Mueller, U. (2006). Executive function and the promotion of social–emotional competence. Journal of Applied Developmental Psychology, 27, 300-309.

Rivara, J.B., Jaffe, K.M., Polissar, N.L., Fay, G.C., Liao, S., & Martin, K.M. (1996). Predictors of family functioning and change 3 years after traumatic brain injury in children. Archives of Physical Medical Rehabilitation, 77, 754-764.

Rocke, K., Hays, P., Edwards, D., & Berg, C. (2008). Development of a performance assessment of executive function: the Children's Kitchen Task Assessment. American Journal of Occupational Therapy, 62, 528-537.

Romine, C.B., & Reynolds, C.R. (2005). A model of the development of frontal lobe functions: Findings from a meta-analysis. Applied Neuropsychology: Adult, 12, 190-201.

Rosema, S., Crowe, L., & Anderson, V. (2012). Social function in children and adolescents after traumatic brain injury: A systematic review 1989-2011. Journal of Neurotrauma, 29, 1277-1291.

Rosen, C.D., & Gerring, J.P. (1986). Head trauma: Educational reintegration. San Diego, CA: College-Hill Press.

Ross, K.A., Dorris, L., & McMillam, T. (2011). A systematic review of psychological interventions to alleviate cognitive and psychosocial problems in children with acquired brain injury. Developmental Medicine & Child Neurology, 53, 692-701.

Rutherford, M.D., Young, G.S., Hepburn, S., & Rogers, S.J. (2006). A longitudinal study of pretend play in autism. Journal of Autism and Developmental Disorders, 37, 1024-1039.

Sady, M.D., Vaughan, C.G., & Gioia, G.A. (2011). School and the concussed youth: Recommendations for concussion education and management. Physical Medicine and Rehabilitation Clinics of North America, 22, 701-719.

Salorio, C.F., Slomine, B.S., Grados, M.A., Vasa, R.A., Christensen, J.R., & Gerring, J.P. (2005). Neuroanatomic correlates of CVLT-C performance following pediatric traumatic brain injury. Journal of the International Neuropsychological Society, 11, 686-696.

Sambuco, M., Brookes, N., & Lah, S. (2008). Paediatric traumatic brain injury: A review of siblings' outcome. Brain Injury, 22, 7-17.

Sandford, A.A., Davidson, T.M., Herrera, N. et al. (2006). Olfactory dysfunction: a sequela of pediatric blunt head trauma. International Journal of Pediatric Otorhinolaryngology, 70, 1015–1025.

Satz, P. (1993). Brain reserve capacity on symptom onset after brain injury: A formulation and review of evidence for threshold theory. Neuropsychology, 7, 273-295.

SCAT2 (2009). British Journal of Sports Medicine, 43, i85-i88.

Schmidt, A.T., Hanten, G.R., Li, X., Orsten, K.D., & Levin, H.S. (2010). Emotion recognition following pediatric traumatic brain injury: Longitudinal analysis of emotional prosody and facial emotion recognition. Neuropsychologia, 48, 2869-2877.

Schneier, A.J., Shields, B.J., Hostetler, S.G., Xiang, H., & Smith, G.A. (2006). Incidence of pediatric traumatic brain injury and associated hospital resource utilization in the United States. Pediatrics, 118, 483-492

Schoenberg, M.R., Lange, R.T., Brickell, T.A., & Saklofske, D.H. (2007). Estimating premorbid general cognitive functioning for children and adolescents using the American Wechsler Intelligence Scale for Children-Fourth Edition: demographic and current performance approaches. Journal of Child Neuropsychology, 22, 379-388.

Schoenberg, M.R., Lange, R.T., Saklofske, D.H., Suarez, M., & Brickell, T.A. (2008). Validation of the Child Premorbid Intelligence Estimate method to predict premorbid Wechsler Intelligence Scale for Children-Fourth Edition Full Scale IQ among children with brain injury. Psychological Assessment, 20, 377-384.

Schwartz, L., Taylor, H.G., Drotar, D., Yeates, K.O., Wade, S.L., & Stancin, T. (2003). Long-term behavior problems following pediatric traumatic brain injury: Prevalence, predictors, and correlates. Journal of Pediatric Psychology, 28, 251-263.

Semrud-Clikeman, M. (2010). Pediatric traumatic brain injury: Rehabilitation and transition to home and school. Applied Neuropsychology: Adult, 17, 116-122.

Sesma, H.W., Slomine, B.S., Ding, R., & McCarthy, M.L. (2008). Executive functioning in the first year after pediatric traumatic brain injury. Pediatrics, 121, 1686-1696.

Shaffer, D., Bijur, P., Chadwick, O.F.D., & Rutter, M.L. (1980). Head injury and later reading disability. Journal of the American Academy of Child Psychiatry, 19, 592-610.

Shoda, Y., & Smith, R.E. (2004). Conceptualizing personality as a cognitive-affective processing system. A framework for models of maladaptive behavior patterns and change. Behavior Therapy, 35, 147-166.

Shum, D., Levin, H., & Chan, R.C. (2011). Prospective memory in patients with closed head injury: A review. Neuropsychologia, 49, 2156-2165.

Simpson, D., & Reilly, P. (1982). Pediatric coma scale. Lancet, 2, 450.

Silver, C.H., Blackburn, L.B., Arffa, S., Barth, J.T., Bush, S.S., Koffler, S.P., et al. (2006). The importance of neuropsychological assessment for the evalutaion of childhood learning disorders NAN Policy and Planning Committee. Archives of Clinical Neuropsychology, 21, 741-744.

Sjö, M., Spellerberg, S., Weidner, S., & Kihlgren, M. (2009). Training of attention and memory deficits in children with acquired brain injury. Acta Pædiatrica 99, 230-236.

Skinner, H.A., Santa-Barbara, J. & Steinhauer, P.D. (1983). The family assessment measure. Canadian Journal of Community Mental Health 2, 91-105.

Slater, E.J., & Bassett, S.S. (1988). Adolescents with closed head injuries. American Journal of Diseases of Children, 142, 1048-1051.

Sohlberg, M.M., Avery, J., Kennedy, M., Ylvisaker, M., Coelho, C., Turkstra, L., & Yorkston, K. (2003). Practice guidelines for direct attention training. Journal of Medical Speech-Language Pathology, 3, 19-39.

Sohlberg, M.M., Johnson, L., Paule, L., Raskin, S.A., & Mateer, C.A. (2001). APT-II: A program to address attentional deficits for persons with mild cognitive dysfunction (An upper extension of the APT-I). Wake Forest, NC: Lash & Associates Publishing/Training Inc.

Sohlberg, M.M., McLaughlin, K.A., Pavese, A., Heidrich, A., & Posner, M. (2001). Evaluation of attention process training and brain injury education in persons with acquired brain injury. Journal of Clinical and Experimental Neuropsychology, 22, 656-676.

Souza, L.M.N, Braga, L.W., Filho, G.N., & Dellatolas, G. (2007). Quality-of-life: Child and parent perspectives following severe traumatic brain injury. Developmental Neurorehabilitation, 10, 35-47.

Spanos, G., Wilde, E., Bigler, E., Cleavinger, H., Fearing, M., Levin, H., et al. (2007). Cerebellar atrophy after moderate-to-severe pediatric traumatic brain injury. American Journal Neuroradial, 28, 537-542.

Spreen, O., & Gaddes, W.H. (1969). Developmental norms for 15 neuropsychological tests age 6 to 15. Cortex, 5, 171–191.

Straus, E., Sherman, E.M.S., & Spreen, O. (2006). A compendium of neuropsychological tests: Administration, norms, and commentary (3rd ed.). New York: Oxford University Press.

Sroufe, L.A., & Fleeson, J. (1986). Attachment and the construction of relationships. In w. Hartrup, & Z. Rubin (Eds.), Relationships and development (pp. 51-71). Hillsdale, NJ: Lawrence Erlbaum Associates.

Sroufe, N.S., Fuller, D.S., West, B.T., Singal, B.M., Warschausky, S.A., & Maio, R.F. (2010). Postconcussive symptoms and neurocognitive function after mild traumatic brain injury in children. Pediatrics , 125, 1331-1340.

Stancin, T., Drotar, D., Taylor, H.G., Yeates, K.O., Wade, S.L., & Minich, N.M. (2002). Health-related quality of life of children and adolescents after traumatic brain injury. Pediatrics, 109, e34.

Stancin, T., Wade, S.L., Walz, N.C., Yeates, K.O., & Taylor, H.G. (2010). Family adaptation 18 months after traumatic brain injury in early childhood. Journal of Developmental and Behavioral Pediatrics, 31, 317-325.

Stancin, T., Wade, S.L., Walz, N.C., Yeates, K.O., & Taylor, H.G. (2008). Traumatic brian injuries in early childhood: Initial impact on the family. Journal of Developmental and Behavioral Pediatrics, 29, 253-261.

Stierwalt, J.A., & Murray, L.L. (2002). Attention impairment following traumatic brain injury. Seminars in Speech and Language, 23, 129-138.

Stuss, D.T. (2007). New approaches to prefrontal lobe testing. In B. Miller, & J. Cummings (Eds). The human frontal lobes: functions and disorders (2nd ed.) (pp. 292-305). New York: The Guildford Press.

Sullivan, J.R., & Riccio, C.A. (2010). Language functioning and deficits following pediatric traumatic brain injury. Applied Neuropsychology: Adult, 17, 93-98.

Sutton, M. (2012). Apps for brain injury rehab. The ASHA Leader, July, 21.

Swift, E.E., Taylor, H.G., Kaugars, A.S., Drotar, D., Yeates, K.O., Wade, S.L., et al. (2003). Sibling relationships and behavior after pediatric traumatic brain injury. Journal of Developmental and Behavioral Pediatrics, 24, 24-31.

Tay, S.Y., Ang, B.T., Lau, X.Y., Meyyappan, A., & Collinson, S.L. (2010). Chronic impairment of prospective memory after mild traumatic brain injury. Journal of Neurotrauma, 27, 77-83.

Taylor, H.G., Swartwout, M.D., Yeates, K.O., Walz, N.C., Stancin, T., & Wade, S.L. (2008). Traumatic brain injury in young children: Postacute efects on cognitive and school readiness skills. Journal of the International Neuropsychological Society, 14, 734-745.

Teasdale, G., & Jennett, B. (1974). Assessment of coma and impaired consciousness. A practical scale. Lancet, 2, 81-84.

Thaler, N.S., Bello, D.T., Carol, R., Goldstein, G., Mayfield, J., & Allen, D.N. (2010). IQ profiles are associated with differences in behavioral functioning following pediatric traumatic brain injury. Archives of Clinical Neuropsychology, 25, 781-790.

Thompson, N.M., Francis, D. J., Stuebing, K.K., Fletcher, J.M., Ewing-Cobbs, L., Miner, M.E., Levin, H.S., & Eisenberg, H.M. (1994). Motor, visual-spatial, and somatosensory skills after closed head injury in children and adolescents: A study of change. Neuropsychology, 8, 333-342.

Tilford, J.M., Aitken, M.E., Goodman, A.C., Fiser, D.H., Killingsworth, J.B., Green, J.W., & Adelson, P.D. (2007). Child health-related quality of life following neurocritical care for traumatic brain injury: an analysis of preference-weighted outcomes. Neurocritical Care, 7, 64-75.

Tlustos, S.J., Chiu, C.Y., Walz, N.C., Taylor, H.G., Yeates, K.O., & Wade, S.L. (2011). Emotion labeling and socio-emotional outcomes 18 months after early childhood traumatic brain injury. Journal of the International Neuropsychological Society, 17, 1132-1142.

Tonks, J., Williams, W.H., Framptom, I. Yates, P., & Slater, A. (2007). Assessing emotion recognition in 9–15-years olds: Preliminary analysis of abilities in reading emotion from faces, voices and eyes. Brain Injury, 21, 623-629.

Touliatos, J., Perlmutter, B.F., & Straus, M.A. (2001). Handbook of family measurement techniques. Thousand Oaks, CA.: Sage Publications.

Tucker, D.M. (1992). Developing emotions and cortical networks. In M.R. Gunnar, & C.A. Nelson (eds.), Developmental Behavioral Neuroscience. The Minnesota Symposia on Child Psychology (Vol. 24) (pp. 75-128). Hillsdale, NJ: Lawrence Erlbaum Associates, Inc.

Turkstra, L.S., Dixon, T.M., & Baker, K.K. (2004). Theory of Mind and social beliefs in adolescents with traumatic brain injury. NeuroRehabilitation, 19, 245-256.

Turkstra, L.S., & Holland, A.L. (1998). Assessment of syntax after adolescent brain injury: Effects of memory on test performace. Journal of Speech, Language, Hearing Research, 41, 137-149.

Turkstra, L.S., McDonald, S., & DePompei, R. (2001). Social information processing in adolescents: Data from normally developing adolescents and preliminary data from their peers with traumatic brain injury. Journal of Head Trauma Rehabilitation, 16, 469-483.

Turkstra, L.S., McDonald, S., & Kaufmann, P.M. (1996). Assessment of pragmatic comunication skills in adolescents after traumatic brain injury. Brain Injury, 10, 329-346.

Turkstra, L., Ylvisaker, M., Coelho, C., Kennedy, M., Sohlberg, M.M., Avery, J., & Yorkston, K. (2005). Practice guidelines for standardized assessment for persons with traumatic brain injury. Journal of Medical Speech-Language Pathology, 13, 9-38.

U.S. Office of Education (1992). Individuals with Disabilities Education Act (IDEA). Federal Register, 57 (189), 44842-44843.

Vakil, E., Blachstein, H., Rochberg, J., & Vardi, M. (2004). Characterization of memory impairment following closed-head injury in children using the Rey Auditory Verbal Learning Test (AVLT). Child Neuropsychology, 10, 57-66.

Vanderploeg, R.D. (1994). Estimating premorbid level of functioning. In R.D. Vanderploeg (Ed.), Clinician's guide to neuropsychological assessment. New Jersey: Lawrene Erlbaum Associates.

Varni, J.W. (2012). Pediatric Quality of Life Scale (Peds QL). Chicago: Author.

Veiel,H.O., & Koopman, R.F. (2001). The bias in regression-based indices of premorbid IQ. Psychological Assessment, 13, 356-368.

Wade, S.L., Borawski, E.A., Taylor, H.G., Drotar, D., Yeates, K.O., & Stancin, T. (2001). The relationship of caregiver coping to family outcomes during the initial year following pediatric traumatic injury. Journal of Consulting and Clinical Psychology, 69, 406-415.

Wade, S.L., Cassedy, A., Walz, N.C., Taylor, H.G., Stancin, T., & Yeates, K.O. (2011). The relationship of parental warm responsiveness and negativity to emerging behavior problems following traumatic brain injury in young children. Developmental Psychology, 47, 119-133.

Wade, S.L., Taylor, H.G., Drotar, D., Stancin, T., & Yeates, K.O. (1998). Family burden and adaptation during the initial year after traumatic brain injury in children. Pediatrics, 102, 110-117.

Wade, S.L., Taylor, H.G., Yeates, K.O., Drotar, D., Stancin, T., et al. (2006). Long-term parental and family adaptation following pediatric brain injury. Journal of Pediatric Psychology, 31, 1072-1083.

Wade, S.L., Walz, N.C., JoAnne, C., Williams, K.M., Cass, J., Herren, L., et al. (2010). A randomized trial of Teen Online Problem Soliving for improving executive function deficits following pediatric traumatic brain injury. Journal of Head Trauma Rehabilitation, 25, 409-415.

Walz, N.C., Yeates, K.O., Taylor, H.G., Stancin, T., & Wade, S.L. (2009). First-Order Theory of Mind skills shortly after traumatic brain injury in 3- to 5-year-old children. Developmental Neuropsychology, 34, 507-519.

Walz, N.C., Yeates, K.O., Taylor, H.G., Stancin, T., & Wade, S. L. (2010). Theory of mind skills 1 year after traumatic brain injury in 6-to 8-year-old children. The British Psychological Society, 4, 181-195.

Ward, E., Green, K., & Morton, A. (2007). Patterns and predictors of swallowing resolution following adult traumatic brain injury. Journal of Head Trauma Rehabilitation, 22, 184–191.

Ward, H., Shum, D., Dick, B., McKinlay, L., & Baker-Tweney, S. (2004). Interview study of the effects of paediatric traumatic brain injury on memory. Brain Injury, 18, 471-495.

Ward, H., Shum, D., McKinlay, L., Baker, S., & Wallace, G. (2007). Prospective memory and pediatric traumatic brain injury: Effects of cognitive demand. Child Neuropsychology, 13, 219-239.

Ward, H., Shum, D., Wallace, G., & Boon, J. (2002). Pediatric traumatic brain injury and procedural memory. Journal of Clinical and Experimental Neuropsychology, 24, 458-470.

Warriner, E.M., & Velikonja, D. (2006). Psychiatric disturbances after traumatic brain injury: Neurobehavioral and personality changes. Current Psychiatry Reports, 8, 73-80.

Warschausky, S., Kay, J.B., Chi, P., & Donders, J. (2005). Hierarchical linear modeling of California Verbal Learning Test-Children's Version learning curve characteristics following childhood traumatic head injury. American Psychological Association, 19, 193-198.

Wassenberg, R., Max, J.E., Lindgren, S.D., & Schatz, A. (2004). Sustained attention in children and adolescents after traumatic brain injury: Relation to severity of injury, adaptive functioning, ADHD and social background. Brain Injury, 18, 751-764.

Wells, R., Minnes, P., & Phillips, M. (2009). Predicting social and functional outcomes for individuals sustaining paediatric traumatic brain injury. Developmental Neurorehabilitation, 12, 12-23.

Welsh, M.C., & Pennington, B.F. (1988). Assessing frontal lobe functioning in children: Views from developmental psychology. Developmental Psychology, 4, 199-230.

Welsh, M.C., Pennington, B.F., & Grossier, D.P. (1991). A normative-developmental study of executive functions: A window on prefrontal function in children. Developmental Neuropsychology, 7, 131-149.

Wilson, B.C. (1992). Neuropsychological assessment of the preschool child. In I. Rapin, & S.J. Segalowitz (Eds.), Handbook of neuropsychology: Vol. 6. Amsterdam: Elsevier Press.

Wilson, K.R., Donders, J., & Nguyen, L. (2011). Self and parents rating of executive functioning after adolescent traumatic brain injury, Rehabilitation Psychology, 56, 100-106.

Winogron, H.W., Knights, R.M., & Bawden, H.N. (1984). Neuropsychological deficits following head injury in children. Journal of Clinical Neuropsychology, 6, 269-286.

Woodward, H., & Donders, J. (1998). The performance of children with traumatic head injury on the Wide Range Assessment of Memory and Learning-Screening. Applied Neuropsychology: Adult, 5, 113-119.

Wozniak, J.R., Krach, L., Ward, E., Mueller, B.A., Muetzel, R., Schnoebelen, S., et al. (2007). Neurocognitive and neuroimaging correlates of pediatric traumatic brain injury: A diffusion tensor imaging (DTI) study. Archives of Clinical Neuropsychology, 22, 555-568.

Wu, T.C., Wilde, E.A., Bigler, E.D., Yallampalli, R., McCauley, S.R., Troyanskaya, M., et al. (2010). Evaluating the relationship between memory functioning and cingulum bundles in acute mild traumatic brain injury using diffusion tensor imaging. Journal of Neurotrauma, 27, 303-307.

Yeates, K.O., Armstrong, K., Janusz, J., Taylor, H.G., Wade, S., Stancin, T., et al. (2005). Long-term attention problems in children with traumatic brain injury. American Journal of Child and Adolescent Psychiatry, 44, 574-584.

Yeates, K.O., Bigler, E.D., Dennis, M., Gerhardt, C.A., Rubin, K.H., Stancin, T., et al. (2007). Social outcomes in childhood brain disorder: A heuristic integration of social neuroscience and developmental psychology. Psychological Bulletin, 133, 535-556.

Yeates, K.O., Lumenstein, E., Patterson, C.M., & Delis, D.C. (1995). Verbal learning and memory following pediatric closed-head injury. Journal of the International Neuropsychological Society, 1, 78-87.

Yeats, K.O., Luria, J., Bartkowski, H., Rusin, J., Martine, L., & Bigler, E. (1999). Postconcussive symptoms in children with mild closed head injuries. Journal of Head Trauma Rehbilitation, 14, 337-350.

Yeates, K.O., Swift, E., Taylor, H.G., Wade, S.L., Drotar, D., Stancin, T., et al. (2004). Short- and long-term social outcomes following pediatric traumatic brain injury. Journal of the International Neuropsychological Society, 10, 412-426.

Yivisaker, M., & Feeney, T. (2007). Pediatric brain injury: Social, sehavioral, and communication disability. Physical Medicine and Rehabilitation Clinics of North America, 18, 133-144.

Ylvisaker, M., Hartwick, P., & Stevens, M. (1991). School reentry following head injury: Managing the transition from hospital to school. Journal of Head Trauma Rehabilitation, 6, 11-22.

Ylvisaker, M., Szekeres, S.F., & Hartwick, P. (1992). Cognitive rehabilitation following traumatic brain injury. In M.G. Tramontana & S.R. Hooper (Eds.), Advances in child neuropsychology (Vol. I, pp. 168-218). New York: Springer.

Yorkston, K.M., Jaffe, K.M., Polissar, N.L., Liao, S., & Fay, G.C. (1997). Written language production and neuropsychological function in children with traumatic brain injury. Archives of Physical Medicine and Rehabilitation, 78, 1096-1102.

Zelazo, P.D., & Müller, U. (2010) Executive function in typical and atypical development. In. U. Goswami (Ed.), The handbook of childhood cognitive development (2nd ed.). Oxford, UK: Wiley-Blackwell.

Zelazo, P.D., Müller, U., Frye, D., & Marcovitch, S. (2003). Study 3: What do children perseverate on when they perseverate? Monographs of the Society for Research in Child Development, 68, 65-72.

Zimmerman, W. D., Ganzel, T. M., Windmill, I. M., Phillips, M., & Nazar, G. B. (1993). Peripheral hearing loss following head trauma in children. Laryngoscope, 103, 87.

Notes